Missionary Stories
with the Millers

Mildred A. Martin

Illustrated by Edith Burkholder

Miller Family

Missionary Stories with the Millers
© 1993 MM
Copyright 2009 Green Pastures Press

All Rights Reserved

Missionary stories for children

Miller Family Series

Printed and bound in USA 10/11, 2009
Softcover edition printed and bound by
Data Reproductions Corporation
Auburn Hills, MI

Hardcover edition printing by
Data Reproductions Corporation
Auburn Hills, MI
and
Country Pines Inc.
Shoals, IN
Binding by
Dekker Bookbinding
Grand Rapids, MI

ISBN 978-1-884377-16-7   Paperback

ISBN 978-1-884377-17-4   Hardcover

Green Pastures Press
50 Green Pastures Lane
Mifflin, PA 17058

List of Chapters

Chapter

page

Intro   The Dollar That Grew   (United States) 5
1.   They Were Not Afraid   (Congo) 10
2.   The Stolen Testament   (Egypt) 15
3.   The Yellow River   (China) 20
4.   Chief Sechele's Daughter   (Africa) 28
5.   He Wasn't Crazy   (Belize) 37
6.   Rain Out of the Ground   (New Hebrides) 43
7.   They Are Going to Kill You!   (Ethiopia) 49
8.   Too Busy Fishing   (China) 57
9.   Mamma Lillian   (Egypt) 62
10.   The Shotgun That Wouldn't Fire   (Mexico) 68
11.   Jim Elliot and the Auca Indians   (Ecuador) 76
12.   The Miracle From the Meadow   (Romania) 83
13.   She Changed Her Mind   (India) 90
14.   The Tiger is Loose!   (Peru) 95
15.   Saved In the Night   (India) 100
16.   The Talking Tortilla   (Mexico) 105
17.   Martyred at Midnight   (Guatemala) 111
18.   A Modern-Day Elijah   (Korea) 119
19.   A Fortress in the Church   (Armenia) 125
20.   Temple Runaway   (India) 130
21.   Only One Page   (Poland) 137
22.   Day Of Disaster   (Alaska) 140
23.   The Boy Who Was Determined   (India) 147
24.   A Dust Pan For Jesus   (South Africa) 153
25.   The Man With the Gospel Papers   (United States) 160
26.   The Missionary Says a Bad Word   (El Salvador) 167
27.   Lost!   (Belize) 175
28.   Through Water and Fire   (Canada) 185
29.   Uncle Ralph and the Moose   (Canada) 195

Go ye therefore, and teach all nations, baptizing them in the name of the Father, and of the Son, and of the Holy Ghost: Teaching them to observe all things whatsoever I have commanded you: and, lo, I am with you alway, even unto the end of the world. Amen. Matthew 28: 19, 20

Author's Note

Although the "Miller" family setting is partly fictional, all of the missionary stories are about real people and based upon incidents which actually happened. Many of the details, however, have been supplied by the author's imagination. For example, we do not know if Ato Desta (chapter 7) was singing a song when his would be murderers were miraculously withheld from harming him; but it is known that the hymn *Take the Name of Jesus with You,* was one of his favorite songs. I have done my best to provide geographical information and backgrounds of "local color" that are authentic and true-to-life.

THE DOLLAR THAT GREW

"My piggy bank is full enough, Mama," Laura announced.

"Is it?" her mother replied vaguely, hands busy in the sink.

"Yes!" the little girl repeated happily. "My piggy bank is full enough, and I want to send *all* the money to buy Bibles for people that don't have any. Like that story you read us last night!"

"Why that would be very nice, Laura!" said Mama, in surprise, looking at her four-year-old daughter.

"See, Mama," Laura bubbled joyfully. "I have all these pennies. Could you count them for me? I want to send them all to the Bible Mission, and get Bibles for poor people who don't know about Jesus."

Mama dried her hands, and took the little plastic piggy bank. It was a very small bank, only about the size of a grown-up's fist, and the coins in it were nearly all pennies. Laura couldn't count very far yet, so Mama helped her. "One hundred and two... one hundred and three!" Mama counted. "Well, Laura, you have enough pennies to make one whole dollar, plus three more cents. So we will trade the hundred pennies for a dollar bill, and put it in an envelope to send to the Bible Mission."

"How many Bibles can they buy with my money, Mama?" Laura asked eagerly.

"Well, I don't know if one dollar can buy a whole Bible," Mama said slowly. Seeing her little daughter's disappointed face, she added: "But your money will surely help, Laura! God will bless your dollar and it will grow."

Laura's brother Timmy had been sitting at the table with his coloring book while Mama counted the pennies. Now he slid quietly from the chair and went upstairs to his bedroom. Timmy's piggy bank was much bigger than Laura's, and there was more money in it! He unscrewed the lid and peered in. There were quarters, and dimes, and even one real dollar bill! Timmy poured the money onto his bed and pushed it around with his fingers.

"Four quarters make a dollar," Timmy thought to himself. He counted out four quarters from the little pile. Then, after a moment's hesitation, he picked up the lone dollar bill, too. Grandpa had just given Timmy that dollar, and it was the only bill he had. But if little Laura could give a whole dollar... *I'm going to give two dollars to help buy Bibles!* Timmy decided.

"What are you doing, Timmy?" asked ten-year-old Peter, looking up from the book he was reading.

"I'm going to give some money to the Bible Mission," his little brother replied, hurrying out of the room with the two dollars clutched in his fist.

After Timmy had gone downstairs, Peter continued to stare at the book in his hands. But instead of the pages of the story, his eyes were seeing the African village his mother had told the children about the night before. The people of that village had been poor, mean, and dirty. But when one of them brought home a Bible, everything changed! They read the Bible and believed in God's love. They cleaned up their village. Now they were happy, healthy, and hard-working, all because of that one Bible!

Peter got up, leaving his book face-down on the bed, and went over to his drawer. He didn't have a piggy bank anymore, but he had a wallet. He opened it and fingered the few bills inside: money he was saving to buy a chemistry set. Peter took out a five dollar bill, and put the wallet back in his drawer. The chemistry set would have to wait a little longer!

"What were you boys saying about the Bible Mission?" Sharon asked Peter as he passed her in the hall.

"We want to send them some of our money to

buy Bibles," Peter explained to his older sister.

"Good!" Sharon replied excitedly. "I'll help, too!" She went to her room and unzipped her purse. *Oh, dear, I don't have much money right now,* she thought. *Except for this...* hesitantly she opened an inner pocket where she had been saving something special. It was a ten dollar bill Sharon had won for a prize in school. *But what could be more special than Bibles?* Sharon thought with a smile. *I'll give this!* she said determinedly, and closed the purse.

Meanwhile, downstairs Mama had been doing some thinking, too. *Dear little Laura, to give all her money for Bibles!* Mama thought. *If we grown-ups do our part so unselfishly too, we can help her dollar grow.* Reaching for her own purse, Mama took out the money she had planned to use for a new dress for herself. *I can wait until next month to buy my dress material,* she thought. *Bibles are more important!*

When Daddy came home that evening, the family showed him their envelope of money for the Bible Mission. "Very good!" he gave his approval." The Lord is pleased when we give. We must pray that He will bless the Bible Mission and help them to send Bibles to those who need them the most." Late that night Daddy sat alone at his desk. The children were in bed, and all was quiet. The envelope addressed to the Bible Mission lay on the desktop, and Daddy's hands were folded above it in silent prayer. *Thank You, God, for little Laura, with her precious little dollar!* he prayed. *She set the example for us all.*

Opening a desk drawer, Daddy reached for his checkbook. He had something to give, too! *God blessed Laura's little dollar, and it grew,* he thought with a smile. *Before I seal up this envelope, it will have grown into one hundred dollars for Bibles.*

"I wish you would tell us some more missionary stories about the Gospel in other countries," Sharon told her mother the next day.

"Yes, Mom! Please find more stories like that and read them to us!" Peter and Timmy begged.

Mrs. Miller smiled at her eager children. "Yes, I will do my best to find you some more stories about missionaries," she promised.

And these are the stories she told them:

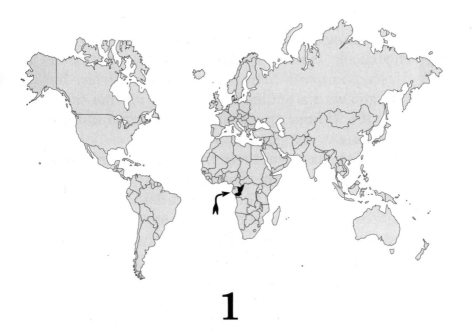

1

THEY WERE NOT AFRAID

With a sudden start, August Eicher jerked awake. For a moment he lay still, staring at the thatch-covered roof poles of his bedroom. What had awakened him?

The faint grey light of dawn was already filtering through the window, but August could hear no sound. What was wrong? *Everything is **too** quiet,* August realized. *Here in the Congo, we are awakened every morning by those noisy weaver-birds screeching in the trees outside our window. But today the birds are silent.*

A sense of danger prickled the hairs on the back of the young missionary's neck. He sat up and reached over to touch his wife. "Wake up, dear," he said softly. "We'd better get dressed; something might be wrong." Mrs. Eicher's eyes fluttered open. "Is it the Simbas?" she whispered sleepily.

The year was 1964, and missionaries in the African country of Congo needed to be very brave. Civil war was ravaging the nation, with wild bands of rebels bursting from their jungle hide-outs to rob and murder wherever they chose. They were mostly young men and boys, idle and lawless, who grouped together with no purpose in life but to terrorize others. "Simba" is the word for "lion" in the Swahili language of Congo, and the terrorists called themselves "Simbas".

Now the missionary couple knelt side by side in their simple bedroom, and prayed for God's grace to meet whatever this new day might bring.

"The sun will soon be up," August observed to his wife when they had risen from their knees. "I'll go start the generator, then we can call one of the other stations and see if there's any news of..."

Crash! August Eicher's words were drowned out by the noise of splintering wood, as the door of the mission house burst open. A blast of automatic gunfire sounded deafeningly close by. "Get out, American spies! Dogs! Pigs!" the intruders shouted in voices full of hatred. Three of them rushed into the room at once and seized August. With one pulling each of his arms and another grasping his neck, they dragged the unresisting missionary out of his house.

"You, too," a fourth man in a leopard-skin cap commanded Mrs. Eicher. *This must be a bad dream,* she thought numbly as she silently followed the men into the yard.

Outside the door she stopped and looked around. An early morning mist was just fading from the valley. The day was going to be clear and sunny, with just a few puffy white clouds to make the blue African sky more vivid. Just beyond the mission house, a hill dropped abruptly, giving a breath-taking view of the deep green jungle valley. Light green banana trees with their huge leaves mingled together with the darker green of dense hardwood trees. Beyond lay the distant ribbon of the river.

But the early morning beauty was spoiled by man's cruelty and sin. August Eicher and his wife were surrounded on all sides by wicked-looking men. Some had whitened their black faces with chalky manioc paste. Goat horns protruded from one man's hat, giving him the appearance of a forest devil. Their bodies were scantily clad in ragged shorts or tattered army uniforms, and each wore a bit of animal skin tied to his cap or around his wrist. Their foreheads above the nose showed fresh cuts where they had gashed themselves with knives. This was the badge of a Simba, the lions of the Congo!

A hiss of horrible triumph rose from the watching men at the sight of their prey. "SSSimba! Simba! Simba!" they chanted in devilish glee. One hard black fist shot out and hit August Eicher in the face, another in his stomach. A trickle of blood ran down his forehead as the two men holding him twisted his arms and forced him to kneel. "Just wait, American pig!" cried a boy, waving a machete. "I'm going to carve you up and eat you!"

"Bring that hammer," ordered the terrorist leader. "We'll smash his head like a rotten egg!"

"Aren't you afraid?" a grinning youth teased, brandishing the heavy sledgehammer he had found in a shed by the mission.

"And you, woman," another fellow turned to the missionary's wife with an evil laugh. "Aren't you afraid of what we will do to you after we kill your husband?"

The sun was rising over the isolated mission station, but the Eichers knew they could not expect any human help to come to them with the daylight. No policemen or soldiers were close enough to rescue them. Their Congolese friends in the small village nearby were all hiding in their huts, trembling with fear of the Simbas. Nothing except the power of God could save these missionaries from the powers of darkness! Yet the power of God was enough.

August Eicher's eyes sought his wife's face, and saw only a mirror of his own faith in God. "No, I am not afraid!" he boldly answered their tormentors. "Our lives are in God's hands. If you kill us, we will go home to be with God."

"No, I am not afraid," repeated his wife, calmly. As she said the words, she knew that she was speaking the truth. All her fear was gone as she looked quietly around the circle of Simbas. These ferocious enemies were only poor, lost souls who needed the Savior!

The missionaries' courage startled their attackers. "Aww, they're no fun," one hideously painted man muttered to another. "We might as well let them go!" An argument began. Some of the Simbas still wanted the blood of the missionaries. Others were ready to spare their lives, but steal what they could from the mission house. For several hours more they talked, disputing among themselves and threatening the Eichers, trying to get them to show fear.

At last the leaders made their decision. "Go into your house quickly," the man with the leopard-skin cap told August. "You have five minutes to gather a few of your personal belongings. Then get out and go to your friends in the village. We are taking over your house, but we have decided to let you go."

Fierce African sunshine beat upon the heads of the missionary couple as they strode down the trail to the village. Although August wanted to run, he was careful to keep a steady, calm pace. A few of the Simbas might yet be watching for any sign of panic. He knew he could still hear the crack of gunfire behind him and feel bullets in his back.

At last the trail turned around a bend, and the mission house was hidden by the forest. August stopped and turned to his wife. Smiles split their faces as they gazed at one another. "Thank God!" August Eicher said simply. "He has saved us from the jaws of the lion."

Historical Note:

Over 100 Christian missionaries were killed during the Congo rebellion in 1964. But August Eicher and his wife were among the many others who were miraculously saved. The Eichers hid in the forest with their Congolese friends for a week, until a missionary pilot came to fly them out to safety. Although the church in Congo suffered much, they stayed true to God! Many of the missionaries who survived came back to their posts as soon as it became possible.

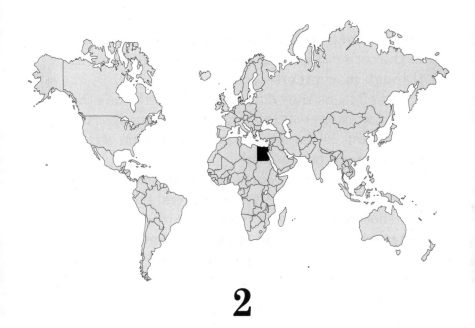

2

THE STOLEN TESTAMENT

Hot sunshine glared down on the white dusty street, but it was dark and cool inside the old-fashioned stone post office building. Noon break was over in this city in Egypt, and all the postal workers were coming back to their job.

Ramsey, one of the postal clerks, rubbed his eyes sleepily and yawned. Slowly he sauntered over to the heavy metal trolley and picked up a canvas sack of mail. Lifting the tag attached by its cord to the mouth of the sack, Ramsey read where the mail in this sack had come from— and suddenly he was wide awake!

This mail sack had come from overseas. Better yet, from rich America! There could be something good here. Ramsey smiled a sly, secretive smile as he carried the canvas bag over to his own desk in the corner. Opening the sack, he began to riffle through its contents.

As often as they could, Ramsey and the other postal workers would steal things from the mail they sorted. Dishonesty didn't bother them, so long as they were not caught!

Now, as Ramsey sorted through the letters in this bag, he kept his eyes open for valuable things. He shook packages to hear what their contents sounded like. He held thinner letters up to the window where the light shining through might reveal money inside.

Halfway through the sack, Ramsey found a special letter which puzzled him. Something thick was in the envelope, and the envelope itself was made of paper too heavy to see through. The packet was addressed to someone Ramsey did not know, a teacher at one of the city schools.

Well, I guess I'll take this one home and open it, Ramsey decided. He ran his fingers casually through his curly black hair. Then, after glancing around the room to make sure nobody was watching, he slipped the letter into the pocket of his uniform jacket.

After work, Ramsey went down the front steps of the Post Office into the heat and dust again. Taxicabs and big buses belching black diesel smoke shared the street with carts pulled by donkeys. Two women in long black robes came by, carrying heavy loads balanced on their heads. Their sandals slapped the dusty pavement as they hurried to get out of Ramsey's way. Not only was he a man, but he also wore the uniform of a Government worker! Clearly he was too important to make way for common peasant women on the narrow sidewalk.

Turning the corner, Ramsey passed a shop that sold oranges and bananas. The oranges hung from the ceiling in mesh bags, where the thieving children couldn't reach them. The bananas, too, swung in huge bunches just as they had been picked from the trees.

Farther down the street, Ramsey passed a car parked at the curb. He couldn't tell what kind it was, because the whole car was shrouded from rooftop to tires in a thick green canvas cover. Parked cars in Egypt often have such covers to protect them from dust and from thieves. Only the wealthiest Egyptians can afford a car at all, and Ramsey looked at this one with covetous eyes. *Someday, I want to have a car!* Ramsey said to himself. He patted his pocket, where the mysterious letter from America lay hidden. What if it were full of money? Enough money to make him rich!

Cement block apartment buildings rose eight and nine stories up toward the brassy sky. The many children who lived in these apartments had no grassy lawns to play on. Narrow porches, with the family laundry hanging from the balcony railings, were their only play yards.

One of these apartments was Ramsey's own home, and now he marched up several flights of stairs. Unlocking his door, he hurried inside and locked it again behind him.

Now, for the packet from America! Carefully

Ramsey slit open one end with his knife, and shook the envelope. Out fell a small, flat book, and Ramsey picked it up.

No money, he decided in disappointment as he leafed quickly through the pages. But what kind of book was *this?* The title on the cover said, in Egyptian: *The New Testament.* Below in smaller letters, were the added words: *of Jesus Christ.*

Ramsey stared, his thoughts whirling. *Jesus Christ?* This must be a Christian book. The Holy Book of the Christians! Ramsey had never had the chance to see such a book before, and he decided to make the most of it. Sitting down, he opened the Book and began to read.

Supper was forgotten as Ramsey became caught up in the story. He soon discovered that this Book was made up of many little books with different names. Matthew, the first book, was all about Jesus and His life, and the things He said.

*So **this** is what the Christians believe?* Ramsey thought with a mixture of scorn and fascination.

The second book, Mark, started all over and told the story of Jesus again. So did the book of Luke, and the book of John. But by the time Ramsey had read the story of Jesus for the fourth time, he believed it!

Like most Egyptians, Ramsey was a Muslim. He had never paid much attention to his religion, except to wonder sometimes whether he really would get to heaven someday. Ramsey and his friends all lied, cheated, and stole whenever they had a chance. Allah would overlook such things, the Muslim mullahs told their people, so long as they did some good deeds too! But now Ramsey was truly frightened about his soul.

Jesus, and God His Father, were holy and knew everything! *What can I do?* Ramsey's heart cried out. He kept on reading the next part, the book of Acts. And suddenly, there were the words he needed! *"What must I do to be saved?"* another man had asked. And Paul had told him, *"Believe on the Lord Jesus Christ and thou shalt be saved"! "Repent and be baptized in the Name of Jesus"!*

Right there in his little apartment in Egypt, Ramsey knelt down and asked Jesus to save him.

"Thank You for the Testament," he prayed, "but I'm sorry that I stole it. Tomorrow I will find some Christians, and buy another Testament for myself. Then I will send this one on to the man who was supposed to get it. I want to be sure he has the opportunity to be saved, too."

Historical Note:

Since Christians in Egypt are sometimes persecuted, we do not know Ramsey's real name or the name of the city where he lives. Ramsey's New Testament came from the World Home Bible League, a mission that sends Bibles all over the world.

Now Ramsey believes in the power of God's Word, and he distributes as many Egyptian Scriptures as the Bible League can send him.

Egypt is a hot, dusty country in Northern Africa, with a population of 55 million people. Most of them are Muslims, like Ramsey was, and need to hear about Jesus.

3

THE YELLOW RIVER

"Look, children! I can see the Yellow River!" The small missionary woman stood on a rocky mountainside in Northern China with a hundred Chinese children straggling around her. The children were tired, filthy, and very hungry. They had been walking through these mountains for twelve days.

"Ai-weh-deh, my feet hurt!"

"Ai-weh-deh, when will you carry me?" "I'm hungry, Ai-weh-deh!"

The smaller children's voices were a chorus of complaint. Most of them were orphans who knew no mother but this Christian missionary, whom they called "Ai-weh-deh".

Ai-weh-deh, "The Virtuous One", bent over

wearily. "Come, Ling, it's your turn to ride," she told a small boy.

When the enemy Japanese marched into their city of Tsechow two weeks ago, she had been wounded by a bullet in her back. Ever since, she had felt so weak and tired! But the children from the mission orphanage must be taken to safety, so Ai-weh-deh had volunteered to lead them through the mountains to the Yellow River. On the other side of the river, there would be a train that could carry the children to another mission in Sian, a safer part of China.

"See, children!" she encouraged the group. "Down there is the village of Yuan Chu, and beyond it is the Yellow River. See it shining in the sunshine!"

"But it's so far away, Ai-weh-deh. And we're so hungry!"

"In the village of Yuan Chu, they will give us food, and then we will arrive at the Yellow River. When we cross the river, we'll all be safe," the missionary answered calmly. "Now let's sing a song as we march down to the town."

The mountains were wild and barren and everyone's thin, homemade cloth shoes were worn out. They had had no food for the last two days, and very little water. Often the rocky slopes were so steep that the bigger children had to form a human chain down the mountainside and pass the younger ones down from hand to hand. But when Ai-weh-deh tried to rally them with a hymn, they would march along, singing bravely.

"I am Jesus' little lamb,

Happy all the day long I am!"

They sang as they followed the path down through the foothills into the town. After sleeping out on the cold hard mountainside for so many days, it was wonderful to see a town and houses!

But as the refugees entered the town, they were in for a disappointment. The town of Yuan Chu had been badly bombed. The streets were littered with rubble from broken houses and nearly all the roofs were gone from the buildings. The whole town was silent, still and empty!

The children ran from house to house, their shrill voices echoing in the deserted streets. "Here's someone, Ai-weh-deh! We found a man!" Two of the older boys called.

The missionary hurried up to the lone old man, sitting beneath a tree. "Old man, this is Yuan Chu, isn't it?" she asked loudly.

"Yes, this is Yuan Chu."

"But where are all the people?"

"They've run away," the old man croaked. "The Japanese soldiers are coming, so everyone went across the Yellow River."

"Why haven't you gone, too?" Ai-weh-deh asked him. "Do you want to come with us?"

"I'm too old to run," the man answered. "I'll sleep here in the sun until the Japanese arrive, and if they kill me, who will care? All my family are dead."

He squinted at the children crowding around him. "Where are all these children from? You are a fool, woman, to bother with so many children. The gods intended for a woman to have only a handful of children, not an army!"

"I am a Christian," the missionary answered quietly, "and my God helps me care for all who need help. How far is it to the river?"

"Three miles," said the old man. "You can follow the road to the ferry, but there will not be any boats there. The Japanese are coming, and everyone else has already crossed the river!"

Ai-weh-deh blew her whistle, and the children lined up around her. "Come, children," she ordered, "it is only a little farther to the river. We shall all bathe and wash our clothes there, and we shall catch a boat and be safe on the other side. Good-bye, old man!" she called, but he had already fallen asleep once more.

The refugees trudged down a dusty path to the river's edge. There were reeds along the bank, and little sandy beaches where the children could splash and paddle in the shallow water. These children, who had grown up in the mountains, had never seen so much water! They ran into it with excited shouts, their hunger forgotten. The river was about a mile wide, running swift and deep in the center. But there was no sign of any boats!

"Where are the boats, Ai-weh-deh?" one of the older children asked.

"They must come across every now and then," she answered. "Maybe we're too late today. We'll spend the night here on the bank, so we'll be ready to meet a boat tomorrow morning."

The children and the missionary huddled together on the sandy bank, as the moon rose above the Yellow River. It was beautiful, quiet and peaceful, but Ai-weh-deh was worried. Why were there no boats? Was the old man right? Had they come too late? When she finally fell sleep, she dreamed of cruel Japanese soldiers in their round steel helmets, marching closer and closer.

When she awoke the next morning, the children were already playing in the water. They explored and poked in the reeds and shallows along the banks, still amazed at the huge river! But curiosity would not fill their hungry bellies for very long. Somehow she must find them food.

She called the oldest boys and told them, "We must look for something to eat! Go back to the town and search the houses. Surely the people left a few scraps of food behind. Look everywhere and bring any food you can find."

The boys headed back to the deserted village and Ai-weh-deh sat on the riverbank. She watched the sun climb up the sky, as it reflected blindingly on the wide stretch of water. If only a boat would come!

The big boys returned, carrying what food they could find: a few pounds of moldy grain in a basket, some dried noodle dough, and several withered peppers and onions. It wasn't much, but they boiled it all together in a big pot of river water over a fire of dried reeds, and carefully rationed out the soup into the children's bowls. When they had all had some there was none left for Ai-weh-deh, but at least the children were fed.

All day, she sat quietly watching the children and listening for the dreaded sound of airplanes that might bring the enemy with their bombs and machine guns. At night, the children whimpered before they went to sleep.

"Ai-weh-deh, we're hungry!"

"Ai-weh-deh, when are we going to cross the river? When are the boats going to come, Ai-weh-deh?"

She prayed then and comforted them as best she could. Surely tomorrow a boat would come!

They ate the last crumbs of food on the third day at the bank of the Yellow River. The children were tired of playing in the water, so Ai-weh-deh told them stories and they sang songs together. Her eyes hurt from staring over the water in search of a boat.

Little Sualan crept close to her. "Ai-weh-deh, remember the story of how Moses took the children of Israel to the Red Sea? And how God opened the water so the Israelites could cross safely?"

"Yes, I remember," the missionary said softly.

"Then why doesn't God open the waters of the Yellow River for us to cross?"

"I'm not Moses, Sualan," she replied, looking sadly at the little girl.

"But God is always God, Ai-weh-deh. You have told us so a hundred times. If God is God, He can open the water for us!"

"Let us kneel down and pray, Sualan," Ai-weh-deh agreed. "We need to have faith! Maybe soon our prayers will be answered."

At that same moment, a small band of Chinese soldiers was creeping along on the same side of the Yellow River. They were scouts, sent by their army to look for signs of the Japanese, and they were frightened and watchful. When darkness fell, they would signal their comrades on the other side of the river, and a boat would be sent to ferry them back to safety. But now, it was their duty to explore the enemy territory. Suddenly, their young officer heard a far-off sound! Was it a plane? He glanced nervously around the cloudless sky. Where were the Japanese planes? Usually they patrolled this stretch of the river, firing their machine guns at anything that moved. But for the past several days there had been no planes.

"That noise isn't a plane," one of his men suggested. "I think it sounds like singing."

The officer crawled cautiously to the top of a hill of sand and lifted his binoculars to peer in the direction of the strange sound. "Wah!" he grunted in surprise.

There on the sandy river bank, was a great crowd of children! They were all seated in a circle, singing loudly. Was this a Japanese trick?

Signalling his men to stay hidden, he walked along the beach toward the children.

Some of the children saw him and shouted with delight. "Ai-weh-deh!" they screamed. "Here's a soldier. A Chinese soldier!"

Then the officer saw a small woman, who rose to meet him. Although she was dark-haired and dressed in Chinese clothing, he knew she was a foreigner, a white woman.

"This will soon be a battlefield," he told her sternly. "What are you doing here? Are you in charge of all these children?"

"Yes, I am in charge of them," Ai-weh-deh replied. "We are waiting to cross the river!"

"I think I can get you a boat," said the officer. "It is small, and we will need to make three trips to take you all across. If a Japanese plane comes by when you are in the middle of the water, they will kill you!"

Standing at the water's edge, the officer put two fingers in his mouth and gave a piercing whistle. From across the river three answering whistles came, and small figures of men appeared with a boat which had been hidden in the reeds.

"I can't thank you enough," the missionary told him. "I thought we were done for, when we couldn't find any boats! You are God's answer to our prayer!"

With shouts of glee, children piled into the boat. The soldiers rowed rapidly to the other side, and then returned for more. On the last trip, Ai-weh-deh and Sualan climbed in together.

"You see, Ai-weh-deh?" chuckled the little girl. "God is always God. He opened the Red Sea, and He can also make a way for us through the Yellow River!"

Historical Note:

Ai-weh-deh and her hundred children escaped from the Japanese soldiers over fifty years ago. The children had many more adventures on their way to the mission in Sian, but they all reached safety at last.

Ai-weh-deh's real name was Gladys Aylward. She was an English woman who spent seventeen years as a missionary in China.

4

CHIEF SECHELE'S DAUGHTER

"There is the King's own hut." Mebalwe pointed to a huge cone-shaped building made of thatch. David Livingstone, the quiet slender missionary, stood at his black friend's shoulder. Silently he studied the capital city of Chief Sechele, in central Africa.

The common people's huts were uniform in size and laid out in orderly patterns, the grass roofs shining golden yellow in the sunlight. The earthen streets were swept clean and beaten hard by the passage of many bare feet.

"Here come the guards to meet us!" David exclaimed. A faint prickle of tension was mixed with his excitement. "Brother, shall we pray?" He said softly to Mebalwe. Briefly, both men bowed their heads as they stood on the trail.

"Thank You, Lord, for moving Chief Sechele to send for us," David prayed. "Help us to win him into Your kingdom."

A dozen muscular guards, with towering plumed headdresses and sharp tasseled spears, escorted the two Christians into the village. Their black faces were somber, and as David walked down the street between the rows of huts, he realized that something was wrong here. "Why are the people so sad?" he asked.

"The chief's only child is dying," came the African's reply.

"I am a doctor," David stated. "Take me to Chief Sechele quickly, and perhaps I will be able to help!"

There were three small fires burning before the chief's hut, and near the middle one squatted the weird, wrinkled figure of the witch doctor. He rocked back and forth and muttered a low chant between his toothless gums. Strange decorations hung from strings all around his neck, waist, and arms: dried snake skins, a leopard's claws, the skull of a dead monkey, and some crocodile teeth. Now he took a pinch of dried herbs from a small antelope-horn cup and threw them into his boiling pot, without looking at the visitors.

"Hail! Sechele, Great Elephant of the Bechuana!" David and Mebalwe politely called out the correct greeting as they approached the chief. Chief Sechele rose from his wooden throne in the doorway of his hut. His face under the headdress of blue heron plumes was stern, and his eyes were troubled. "I have sent for you, White Doctor," he announced, "because I have heard that you are skilled in healing. I command you to give my daughter some medicine."

"I will be glad to do whatever I can," David answered simply. "But it is God in heaven Who does the healing. Where is your daughter?"

The witch doctor jumped to his feet and glared resentfully at David. "O Great Chief Sechele," he whined. "I am ready to give your daughter my strongest medicine! We do not need any help from this foreigner. If he touches your daughter, she will surely die!"

An expression of fear flitted across the face of Sechele, but he stood firm. "Come," he told David, and the missionary doctor followed him into the big hut.

As David's eyes adjusted to the dim light inside, he could see the form of a little girl lying on a rug made of leopard skins. Her knees were drawn up to her belly, and she moaned in pain as her mother and several other women stood helplessly by.

"Where does it hurt, Princess?" David asked softly. With gentle hands he felt her feverish head and examined the sore stomach. Then he turned to Chief Sechele. "Her appendix is infected," he told the father. "It is a small thing inside her belly that has become bad. Now I must cut her belly and remove the appendix quickly, before it bursts open and kills her. See," and David opened the pouch of medical equipment he always carried, "here I have a small sharp knife. And with this medicine," he held up a tiny bottle, "I will put her to sleep so she will feel no pain. Then I will close the hole in her side with these," he held up a needle and thread, "and in a few days, she will be well again."

The women gasped at the sight of the knife and began to wail and cry. Chief Sechele frowned. "If you kill my child, I will kill you!" he growled.

"If I don't cut out the bad thing, she *will* die," David pleaded. Seeing that Sechele was wavering, he added, "If she dies, I die too. All right?"

Slowly the chief nodded his head in a gesture of agreement. "Do the thing quickly," he whispered harshly.

David stepped out of the hut into the blinding sunlight once more and beckoned to Mebalwe. "My instruments must be cleansed in the hot water," he told his companion. "While they are boiling, let us pray."

"Are you sure you should take this chance?" Mebalwe questioned softly in English. "If you fail, we will be killed like dogs."

"I believe this opportunity is from the Lord," David replied confidently. "With His help, the operation will succeed. Then Sechele's tribe will be open to the Gospel at last!"

Together the men knelt beside the fire. Hundreds of curious eyes were upon them as David and Mebalwe bowed their heads. "Almighty Lord God," David prayed, "Give my hands the skill to do this operation successfully. Please grant healing to the daughter of Sechele, so that all his people may know You are the one true God!"

The Africans crowded in closely around as

David bent over his little patient. Carefully he gave her just two drops of laudanum from the small bottle, then picked up his sharp knife. Quickly he cut a small gash deep into the child's belly, and removed the diseased appendix. "Just in time," he murmured to Mebalwe. "This thing was about ready to burst!" He closed the cut he had made and bandaged it lightly, then felt the little girl's pulse.

"I have finished," he said to Chief Sechele. "The child will sleep awhile longer. When she awakens, we will know how she is."

One by one the curious onlookers left the hut, to take their own naps in the heat of the day. Chief Sechele and his wife squatted on one side of their sleeping daughter, while David kept watch at the other side. They did not speak, and as David sat silently, his mind ran back over the events that had brought him here to this place.

He thought of his boyhood in Scotland. His parents had been so poor that David had needed to leave school and go into a factory to work at the age of ten. From six o'clock in the morning until eight at night, he had worked in a hot room in the spinning mill, mending broken places in the cotton ropes. He had been responsible to watch one hundred and sixty ropes at once, and often needed to walk more than twenty miles a day as he hurried around and around the whirring machines. In every spare moment, though, he had read all the books he could; especially books about science, and travel in other countries! At the age of twenty, he had decided to become a missionary doctor...

David raised his head now and looked at the sleeping girl, daughter of an important chief. Sechele had been angry and threatening toward the Christian missionaries until now. Would the operation save his daughter's life, and open his tribe's hearts to the Gospel of Jesus?

David gently counted the heartbeats once more as they passed through the child's limp wrist. All seemed to be well and he sat back again with closed eyes to rest and wait. Also to remember another time when his courage had been tested by great danger!

Lions had been terrorizing a little African village close to the mission, and the people had appealed to David for help. "If we can kill one of them, the rest will leave this area," they told the missionary. "Will you come with us?" David had agreed, and that night the men formed a circle. David and Mebalwe had guns, the others held spears. Everyone was silent and tense as the clouds drifted back and forth in front of the moon. Lions had crept toward the cattle pens, then charged the ring of men. David had fired at a lion, then reached down to reload his gun. Suddenly Mebalwe shouted a warning! Out of the darkness the wounded lion rose up right in front of David! It reared over him like a cat pouncing upon a mouse, with the ruff of its enormous mane fully erect. In the light of the flaming torches, its eyes glowed a bright ferocious gold. The lion opened its jaws and roared an ear-shattering gust of sound. David's own yell was lost in the roaring of the enraged animal. He had one glimpse of long,

34

white, cruel fangs in that gaping red mouth and then the charging beast's jaws closed upon David's shoulder. Growling horribly, the four hundred pound lion shook the missionary as a dog shakes a rat!

The remaining lions broke through the circle of screaming men and vanished into the darkness, as Mebalwe fired his gun into the air. Instantly the lion that was attacking David dropped him and sprang at Mebalwe instead, only to fall dead at last on the bloody sand.

David smiled, remembering. *That time the doctor had to have the operation himself,* he thought. He had needed to give directions to the African Christians as they sewed up his wounds and set the splintered bones in his shoulder. *But God kept me alive to work for Him,* David mused. *And now I am trusting God to keep this child alive, too.*

Sechele's daughter stirred on the leopard-skin rug and her eyes fluttered open. "Mother?" she asked weakly. "Father? I'm thirsty." David felt her forehead. It was cool! Her heartbeat was strong and steady. There was gladness in David's eyes as they met the eyes of Chief Sechele. "Give thanks to God," he said triumphantly. "Your daughter will live!"

The Chief rose to his feet. "Come," he told David in a husky voice. "I will have my servants bring you food. After we have eaten, then you shall tell me all about your God. I am ready to listen."

Historical Note:
  David Livingstone was one of the grandest missionary heroes of all time. He spent 33 years in Africa as a pioneer explorer, travelling many

thousands of miles in places where no white man had ever been before.

Africa in those days, the mid-1800's, was called "The Dark Continent", because no one had ever made any maps of it or had any knowledge of its geography. David Livingstone blazed the trail, opening the country to Christianity. Many new mission stations were later planted all through the regions of Africa where David had explored.

Chief Sechele did believe, was converted and baptized. As soon as possible, he learned to read, and became a missionary to his own people.

Mebalwe, who saved David from the lion, was a close friend of David's for the rest of his life. He also was an able preacher who brought many of his people to Christ.

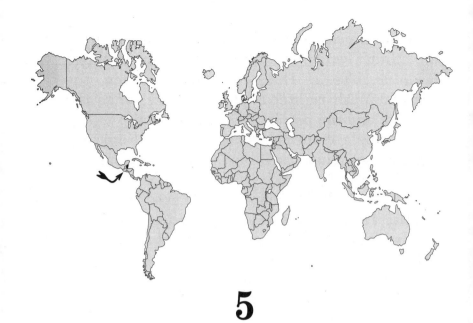

5

HE WASN'T CRAZY

"Look at that Mistah Walker," whispered a young man in flashy clothing to the woman beside him. "I think he's gone crazy!"

The woman took a sip of her whiskey cocktail and giggled as she looked where her boyfriend was pointing. Behind the bar stood the owner himself, a huge black man. Usually Ludlow Walker had a jolly grin and a joke for every customer! But today his face seemed to be distraught with fear. Great drops of sweat rolled down his forehead as he stared at the Book in his hand. His lips moved feverishly, reading the words from the yellowed pages.

"Hey, man! Whatcha got there?" came the raucous voice of a customer on one of the bar stools.

"What are you reading, man?"

"Don't bother me," Ludlow murmured. "Where was I?... Yes... 'The Lord cometh to judge the earth. With righteousness shall he judge the world, and the people...'" he read aloud.

A ripple of uneasiness swept over the crowd of drinkers. "That's a Bible!" muttered someone. "He's crazy, for true!"

"Hey, Ludlow! Come here, I'll give you a cigarette. That will make you feel better!" teased a lady. "Come on, Mistah Walker, turn on some dance music!" someone else shouted. A man in an expensive suit slipped his own full glass along the counter top toward Ludlow. "Here, man," he said softly. "Drink this quickly; you need it worse than I do!"

Ludlow Walker raised his head and looked full in the face of his friend. "No," he spoke deliberately. "I won't drink that. I will never drink liquor again."

A snort of laughter rose from several of the customers, but most sat in horrified silence. "Crazy," someone muttered. "What's going on? Let's get out of here!" He headed for the door, and one by one the other drinkers followed him.

Alone at the bar, Ludlow read on. He could not explain the mysterious sense of conviction which had gripped him that afternoon and caused him to search for this old Bible among his dead father's treasures. He didn't know much about God's plan of salvation, but he knew that he wanted God in his life. *Lord, help me!* he prayed. *I want Your power to change me! I've*

38

had enough of sin and darkness.

At last, secure in the knowledge that God had heard him, Ludlow went to his bed. In the morning, he awoke with a prayer in his heart! "Lord, what shall I do next?"

"You must find other Christians," came the answer from God.

The missionaries, Ludlow thought immediately. *Those Mennonite missionary ladies in the village, who give away free eyeglasses to the poor. I will go talk to them!*

Two days later, Ludlow made his way to the door of the little mission house and soon he was telling Nancy and Alta Coblentz, the mission sisters, about his experience. "Everyone said I was crazy," he finished with a chuckle. "But *you* don't think I've lost my mind, do you?"

"No, indeed!" Nancy Coblentz replied firmly. "You haven't lost your mind— your mind has been renewed! That is what God does for us. We have been praying for you, Mr. Walker, and God has answered our prayer!"

She called for the pastor of the church, Brother Gilbert Stevens, who explained more to Ludlow about the way of salvation. How the Christians rejoiced, as they spoke with this new brother in the Lord!

But not everyone was happy with the news. When Ludlow Walker's friends and customers heard of the change in his life, they were disappointed and angry. Ludlow's motel and bar were famous throughout the country! Government leaders, tourists, and rich businessmen loved to sit and drink in his popular, colorful cocktail lounge. Was Ludlow going to close the place down? What would happen next?

Many people mocked and laughed at Ludlow. "He won't last long," they scoffed. "He loves money too much. He can't give up that nice business. Surely not!"

One afternoon a rowdy group of men came and demanded rooms in the motel. They were drunken and dangerous, and their leader began to threaten Ludlow. "When I'm like this, it's easy for me to kill people!" he growled. "I'm going to get you, if you don't give up your crazy idea of being a Christian and closing this place!"

Ludlow shuddered. This was serious! "Lord," he prayed, "I'm scared. Help me! Show me some sign that you are with me."

The evening sky had been perfectly clear before Ludlow prayed, but suddenly it was full of black clouds. Thunder boomed and forked lightning exploded close by.

The hostile man was astonished and frightened. "You did that, man!" he gasped, looking at Ludlow with eyes full of superstitious fear. "I saw you pray!" Picking up his liquor bottle, he backed away.

Ludlow laughed triumphantly. "No, I didn't do it," he replied. "God did!"

Crack! Lightning struck again, and huge drops of rain began to fall.

The angry, drunken man suddenly seemed quite sober. Turning away, he ran to his room and slammed the door.

"Come back!" Ludlow cried, hurrying after him. "Don't you want to come out and see what else God can do?" But there was no reply. Inside the locked room, the man and his friends had switched off their lights and were huddled fearfully in the darkness together.

Ludlow knelt alone on the sun deck and gave thanks to God. At once, the rain and thunder stopped! All the black clouds slipped away, revealing a fresh, beautiful moonlit sky. Rejoicing at the way God had protected him, Ludlow went home to his bed.

At daybreak, the men who had threatened him quietly sneaked away. When Ludlow returned to his motel in the morning, he stood silently looking around the empty bar room. "Lord," he questioned softly, "what shall I do with all this? If I sell it, or even give it away, it will cause other people to sin." Even as he prayed, Ludlow knew the answer.

Chuckling, he picked up an armload of half-empty liquor bottles and strode outside, where he called for the motel janitor. "Here's some weed killer!" Ludlow told his workman. "We're going to pour it all out on the grounds and driveway, wherever there are weeds." Before the surprised man could reply, his boss had gone back for another load.

As hundreds of dollars' worth of expensive liquors gurgled out onto the ground, a crowd of curious people gathered to watch. "What is he doing?" "He's crazy!" they muttered. The evil drinks sparkled in the sunshine and Ludlow

Walker laughed happily.

"We are getting rid of the devil's poison," he explained to the people. "It will kill the weeds, so what do you think it does to the folks that drink it?"

Shaking their heads, the onlookers drifted away. A few days later they came back to stare again at the strange sight of Ludlow and some workmen tearing down the whole building! With sledgehammers and crowbars, they separated cement blocks and boards. Piece by piece, the famous cocktail lounge was being ripped apart! "We will sell it all for scrap," the owner said with a satisfied smile. "Poor folks may use the pieces to build houses, but no one will ever drink liquor here again."

*   *   *

"Did you hear the latest about Ludlow Walker?" asked one villager of his neighbor a few years later. "He's a minister now!"

The other man sighed. "We all said he was crazy, but I guess God changed him," he added wistfully. "Wouldn't you sort of like to have what he has?"

Historical Note:
Ludlow Walker was a wealthy man who lived in Hattieville, Belize, in 1980. He was obsessed with making more and more money. Someday, he believed, he would be one of the world's richest men! But one day Ludlow realized that money was not bringing him happiness, only greed and fear. In his torment and disappointment, he reached for his father's old Bible, where he found the answer to his questions.

Today Ludlow Walker is the pastor of a church in Southern Florida. He also runs a mission called "Ship Watch" in the great seaport of Miami, where merchant ships come from all over the world. Brother Ludlow and groups of volunteers preach, sing, witness, and give away Bibles and tracts in many languages to the sailors.

6

RAIN OUT OF THE GROUND

"But how can you bring up rain out of the ground, Missi John?"

Old Chief Namakei could not imagine such a strange thing. His dark brown face was wrinkled with worry as he faced the white man. John Paton, the missionary, rolled up his sleeves and lifted the shovel.

"God has put good water down in the ground as well as in the clouds, Chief Namakei," he explained patiently. "We will dig a hole down to find it. Then your people won't need to pay the witch doctor for drinking water."

"Rain out of the ground? Drinking water underground?" a murmur of laughter swept through the watching crowd of natives. The island of Aniwa

43

had no springs, and its people had never heard of fresh water coming from any place except the rain-water cistern on the witch doctor's land. Rain in these New Hebrides Islands was scarce enough, and all that fell soon sank into the dry soil. The only pool of rainwater was closely guarded by the wicked witch doctor. Since he controlled the supply, all the people must pay what he asked or go thirsty! He pretended to be in charge of the weather too, and would do his rain dances only when the people were desperate enough to bring huge offerings to him.

Now the witch doctor lurked in the bushes on the edge of the clearing, keeping an eye on the people as they watched Missionary John. "I will curse them all!" he muttered angrily, fingering his necklace of bat's bones and shark's teeth. "I will curse their yam gardens and their fish traps! I will bring poisonous snakes upon them, until they are ready to forget about this foolish foreign missionary. Fresh water out of the ground, indeed!" He shook his head, making his wooden earrings dance.

"When we have our well of water," John Paton told the people, "it will be free for everyone. There will be enough water for all, to fill your gourds and buckets whenever you wish! Now who will help me dig?"

"Not me! Digging is women's work," laughed a tall young savage with blue designs tattooed all across his muscular chest.

"I'll help for awhile, if you give me one of those sharp metal fish hooks you brought," another man bargained.

Sweat began to roll down the missionary's forehead as he dug busily. "Yes, every man who works for a day may have a fish hook," he replied. "It might take a few days before we reach the water in the ground."

The soil was hard and full of rocky coral, so John Paton was glad when a few men took turns with him in digging. Sitting under a tree to rest, he thought of his boyhood home in Scotland. Scotland was much cooler than the Island of Aniwa, and there was plenty of water there! But John Paton had made up his mind when he was only a little boy, that as soon as he grew up he would be a missionary. These islands of New Hebrides were the place to which God had called him, so here he would stay!

He had found the people to be cannibals, who lived in poor little huts and worshiped almost everything: the shark gods, tree gods, ocean gods, and weather gods. Women did all the work, while the men spent their time in fighting one another. John could not even count the narrow escapes he had had in the past few years: times when his life was almost brought to an end by an axe or gun in savage hands.

Sometimes he had saved himself by running straight into the arms of some cannibal, hugging his enemy tightly to keep him from lifting his club to strike. Once he had knocked up the barrel of a musket aimed at his heart, sending the bullet harmlessly into the air. One night he needed to climb a tall tree and spend the long dark hours hiding in the branches, while savages whooped and fired their muskets below him. Often his life had been saved by nothing but the miraculous power of God, when his attackers were frightened away by angel guardians.

One night, when an army of attacking cannibals burned the mission church, John Paton and the other missionaries were rescued by a ship from another island. After this John had made a trip back to Scotland to raise money for a mission boat of his own. Most of the money came from children in Sunday Schools, and John named the boat "Dayspring". When the beautiful little ship Dayspring returned to the New Hebrides Islands, the savages were filled with surprise.

"How is this?" they marveled. "We killed some of the missionaries and drove the others away. Yet they come back! And not to make money, like other white men. These came only to tell us of their God and His Son Jesus. If their God makes them so brave, we ought to worship Him too!"

Now John Paton was well accepted on the island of Aniwa. He spent much of his time caring for the sick where there were no doctors or nurses. As he walked from one place to the next, he sang hymns in the language of the people of Aniwa. "Missi John!" "Missi John!" children would cry with delight when he passed. *If only I can give the people their own well,* John thought, *then the witch doctor's hold on them will be broken at last!*, and he climbed into the deepening hole once more.

But late in the afternoon, disaster struck. One side of the well hole suddenly caved in and a pile of dirt tumbled down around the feet of the man who was digging. It was not at all dangerous, but the people of Aniwa were terrified. "You see!" the witch doctor shrieked in triumph. "You have made the earth gods angry! This work must stop, or everyone will die!" And nobody could be persuaded to dig another shovelful.

"Then I will dig it by myself," John said sadly. And he toiled on alone, while the people begged him to give up the job. "If you do reach water," they told him, "you will fall through into the sea and the sharks will eat you! Please stop, Missi John!"

Still he dug away, until his hands were blistered by the shovel. A second day, and a third. His hopes rose as the hole grew deeper, for the coral and earth were becoming damp! "I think God will give us water tomorrow," he told the curious watchers as he climbed out of the hole that evening.

Early the next morning, John went down into his well and dug a small hole in the bottom. Suddenly, water came gushing in! John was so excited that he could hardly steady his hand to hold his cup. Dipping the cup full, he tasted the water and found it fresh and sweet!

"Water!" he shouted. "The water is coming in!"

Men, women, and children, all the people of Aniwa came running pell-mell to see the marvelous sight. As the water level rose in the new well, John leaned down to fill his cup again. "You first," he said, handing the cup to Chief Namakei.

At first the old chief dared not touch it. "Yes, it certainly *looks* like rain," he ventured cautiously.

Finally he accepted the cup, shaking it a little to see whether it would spill. Next he had to test the water with his finger. At last he got up enough courage to taste a sip, rolling it around in his mouth. He swallowed, then shouted, "Rain! Rain! Yes, it is rain! Missi John has brought us rain out of the ground!"

Cups of water were passed from hand to hand, and the islanders came one by one to peer wonderingly into the hole which was now full of water.

Chief Namakei stood straight and tall. "Hear me, my people!" he spoke solemnly. "The God who could give us this water is the only true God. I command that all the idols in our houses shall be burned. We will hear Missi John now, and learn all we can about God and His Son Jesus!"

John Paton bowed his head, a prayer of thanksgiving rising in his heart. "Thank You, Lord!" he whispered joyfully.

In the distance, the sad figure of the witch doctor could be seen slipping silently away, all alone, to his hut.

Historical Note:

The well John Paton dug was more of a miracle than he realized that day! In later years when other men tried to dig wells on the island of Aniwa, they could find no fresh water anywhere! Only salty ocean water came up in the wells. The well John dug was the only spot where drinkable water could be found on the island of Aniwa.

John Paton worked as a missionary for nearly 50 years in the New Hebrides Islands.

Chief Namakei also became a Christian minister and preached to his people until his death a few years after this story.

7

THEY ARE GOING TO KILL YOU!

Clang! Clang! CLANG! Ato Desta swung the iron bar in his hand, striking it against the big iron plate.

Clang! Clang! CLANG! He struck three more blows, until the iron plate vibrated on it's rope. The sound of Ato Desta's crude bell rang out over the desert hills of Central Ethiopia. All who heard, knew that the Nazareth Mennonite Mission Hospital was open for the morning!

Leaving his iron bar under the acacia tree where the iron bell hung suspended from a branch, Ato Desta picked up his cane and shuffled across the dusty Mission compound back to his post at the gate.

Although he was not an old man, Ato Desta's

face and body bore the marks of suffering. He had been only a little boy when enemy soldiers had caught and tortured him, trying to find out where more of his people were hiding. But Ato Desta would not tell, no matter what the soldiers did to him! Some of the scars from that terrible day could still be seen on his body. There were no scars, though, in Ato Desta's soul! Living for Jesus brought him such joy, it seemed that his leathery brown face was always wreathed in smiles.

"Desta" means "happiness" in the Amharic language of Ethiopia, and Ato Desta was always happy. He sang now, as he returned to the gate of the hospital compound. The mission doctor, buttoning his white coat as he walked to his office, called a cheery greeting. "Good morning, Ato Desta!" Three nurses scurried past on their way to the hospital building, and young Brother Byler, the new American missionary, came carrying his carpentry tools. "Good morning!"

"Good morning!" Ato Desta repeated happily

Even at 7:30 in the morning, the sun was hot as Ato took his place in the gateway. He had unlocked the gate an hour before, and a few patients had already gathered to wait in the dusty courtyard. A mother carried a sick baby folded within her *shamma*, the long shawl of thin cotton worn by country people in Ethiopia. An elderly blind man, led by his wife, squatted beside a boy with ugly sores on his skin.

Ato Desta was neither a doctor nor a preacher, but he cared about the souls of all the people who came through his gate. He wanted them to know the joy that Jesus had brought to his own heart! Usually he managed to speak a few words to each one about the Lord. Drawing a well-worn New Testament from the pocket of his baggy trousers, Ato went over now to join the blind man and his wife. "Did you ever hear the story of how Jesus healed a blind man?" he asked them quietly.

As the morning wore on, the wiry little gate-keeper was busy. His cane was always ready to deal with any snake, stray dog, or wandering goat that might try to enter the gates of the mission. His dark face was kind as he kept order among the waiting patients. Just before noon, there was a stir of excitement as a man was brought through the gate in a wheelbarrow, his family crowding in after him. The man was a farmer, who had been bitten by a snake as he herded his goats among the scrub. He moaned with pain, his swollen leg hanging over the side of the wheelbarrow.

Ato Desta hurried to help. "Let him through, please!" he called to the crowd of curious people. Taking the wheelbarrow handles from a tired rela-tive, Ato himself pushed the primitive ambulance up the walk toward the emergency room.

"We will have the doctor look at him right away," he assured the anxious family. "Bitten by a snake, was he? Too bad! Snakes are just like the devil, hiding and trying to trap us into sin."

Several men were standing idly in the mission courtyard, watching, and one of them scowled at the words of Ato Desta.

"He preaches a sermon about everything!" growled the man to his friend. He turned and spat

51

disgustedly into the dust. "I'm getting sick of his Christian talk!"

"Yes, now you see what I mean," the other man muttered. "Some of us think it's time to do something about him!" and he glanced furtively around to see whether anyone else had overheard.

The following afternoon, Ato Desta sat dozing in the shade of the brick wall. It was the hottest part of the day, when all Ethiopians stop their work to rest. Suddenly a shadow fell across Ato's cane. Always alert, the gatekeeper straightened quickly. "Good afternoon, Abu!" he greeted the boy who stood beside him. "Are you well today?"

Abu glanced over his shoulder uneasily, then squatted beside Ato Desta.

"There's something I must tell you," he began in a whisper. "Last night I heard my uncle Zodie talking, with two other men. They were drinking a lot, and swearing, and they said—" the boy looked around fearfully once more. "They are going to kill you, Mr. Desta! Tonight, or some night soon when you go home from the hospital, they will be waiting! But please, don't tell anyone that I told you, or my uncle will—" Abu stopped talking as the sound of footsteps was heard behind them in the gateway.

Ato Desta looked up, but saw only an old woman and a child. "It's time to ring the bell for the afternoon clinic," he said, rising to his feet. "Would you like to ring the bell, Abu?"

The boy's face brightened, but he shook his head. "I'd better leave, before someone sees me with you," he worried.

"Well, thank you for coming," Ato Desta told the boy. "And don't be afraid. God will take care of me. I am His, so there is nothing to fear."

Slowly the sun slid down toward its setting place in the Western hills. Ato Desta went about his afternoon with his usual cheerful face, but often his mind went back to Abu's words: "They are going to kill you! Maybe tonight, Mr. Desta!"

Why ever should anyone want to kill me? Ato wondered. *I have no enemies, surely!* His thoughts went to his wife at home, and their little son Johannes. *Lord,* Ato prayed, *My life is Yours. Please be with me and keep me safe according to Your will. If I do have enemies that want to harm me, help them to repent and be delivered from their sin.*

When six o'clock came, Ato Desta's workday at the mission hospital was over. He handed the keys to the night gatekeeper, and picked up his cane and goatskin bag. "Good evening!" he called over his shoulder as he started down the path.

The sun had set, and the evening breezes were cool. Ato walked faster, thinking of home and supper. The road he took was only a rocky footpath, winding among the desert hills. Deep gullies and ditches ran alongside the path, and Ato knew there were snakes and hyenas in them. But these were dangers he was used to facing daily! Surely, no other danger waited on this quiet evening.

Ato Desta prayed again, until his mind was at rest. Throwing his head back, he began to sing joyfully a favorite hymn:

"Take the Name of Jesus with you,

Child of sorrow and of woe.
It will joy and comfort give you,
Take it then where ere you go."

Farther along the path, three men hiding in the ditch heard the sound of singing. "Here he comes!" hissed Zodie.

"That's him, all right; singing his everlasting songs," growled his tall friend Gaytacho. "We'll see if he's still so happy when we jump out on him!"

"Yes, his preaching will stop now," Girma chuckled evilly. "My club will take care of that!" He shook the heavy wooden club in his right hand, then laid it down to pick up his bottle of home-made beer.

"Precious Name, O how sweet!
Hope of earth and joy of heaven!"

Ato Desta's voice rang out over the lonely hills. He was steadily coming closer to the ditch where death waited to silence his joyful witness.

"Is your gun loaded, Gaytacho?" Zodie whispered hoarsely. "Hush! Don't scare him away now," the tall man frowned.

"Don't worry, he's singing too loudly to hear us. My axe is sharp and ready!" boasted Zodie. "No one will ever know what happened to Ato Desta!"

"Take the Name of Jesus ever,
As a shield from every snare...!"

The singer on the path was almost directly above the waiting men.

Girma clenched his fist around his club and tensed, ready for a word from the leader.

"Now!" Zodie's voice exploded beside his ear.

Gaytacho, gun in hand, gathered his muscles to spring up the rocks to the path above. But nothing happened! As if in a dream, he willed himself to move... and could not! His gun suddenly seemed too heavy to lift, his bones as soft as butter. Girma, too, tried to move and couldn't. His arm, holding the club, hung heavy as lead at his side. Bewildered and terrified, he could only roll his eyes to look at his companions. Zodie's usually cocoa-brown face had turned sickly gray with fear. Drops of sweat rolled down as he vainly tried to free himself from the unseen hand that held him prisoner.

"At the Name of Jesus bowing,
Falling prostrate at His feet.
King of kings in Heav'n we'll crown Him,
When our journey is complete!"

Ato Desta sang triumphantly. He was passing by, never suspecting that three enemies listened helplessly. They could not move! The power of Jesus' Name had delivered their prey from the death they had planned for him. When at last their bodies were loosed and they could move again, Ato Desta had disappeared around the next hill. It was too late to attack.

"Precious Name, O how sweet!
Hope of earth and joy of heaven."

Ato Desta repeated the chorus for the last time. He could see his home in the distance: a little house with walls made from mud and sticks, with thatch for the roof. A house full of love and happiness! And there came little Johannes, running to meet his father.

"Here I am, my son!" he called joyfully. Ato

Desta arrived home safely that night... and every night thereafter.

Historical Note:

Ato Desta's miraculous escape took place sometime in the 1950's. Some of the names have been changed. The Nazareth Mennonite Mission hospital is still in operation, though it is now called the Haile Mariam Memorial Hospital.

Brother Byler, the American missionary mentioned in the story, is the author's uncle. He and his wife served in Ethiopia during the 1950's, and personally knew Ato Desta.

8

TOO BUSY FISHING!

It was a warm, windy afternoon on the east coast of China. A breeze rippled the blue waters of the China Sea into little waves that lapped against the muddy shore.

Here and there, boats bobbed on the waves. There were tiny letter-boats, which darted swiftly along, paddled by two men. There were sampans, houseboats where whole families lived and worked and slept in small cabins under the sail. There were little fishing boats, full of dark-winged cormorants with rings around their necks, trained to catch fish for their masters.

Down a little farther along the coastline was a larger fishing boat, where half a dozen men worked with their net. Biggest of all, though, was the hong-boat, a Chinese passenger junk.

As the brawny boat man stood at his tiller, guiding the ship, his passengers sat comfortably under the shelter of the awnings drinking tea and chatting with one another.

At first glance, all of the passengers appeared to be Chinese, too. But a closer look showed that two of the men, though dressed in Chinese clothing and speaking Chinese, were certainly white men. Hudson Taylor, one of the two missionaries, was talking earnestly with the Chinese gentleman beside him.

"You say you have heard the story of Jesus, and you think it sounds like a good teaching," said Hudson Taylor. "But it is not enough to think on Jesus in your mind! You need Jesus in your heart, my friend."

Tears stood in the eyes of the Chinese man. "I must have more time to think of these things," he murmured. "I am not yet ready to decide. I will listen to you preach when we arrive at Sungkiang."

"I can see Sungkiang up ahead!" called John Jones, the other missionary. Several of the passengers stood up to look. Sungkiang was a large city and there were crowds of people to be seen on the shore, streaming toward its gates.

"I'm going down into the cabin, to get our tracts and books ready," Hudson told his fellow missionary. "We will soon have a chance to preach for many people!"

Hudson Taylor was just opening the boxes of Gospel tracts which he carried, when suddenly he heard a tremendous splash and a scream. Dashing out of the cabin, he sprang back onto the main deck. "What happened?" he asked.

"That man fell overboard!" the other missionary cried. "The man you were just witnessing to! I don't think he can swim; most of these people can't."

The other Chinese on the boat stood looking helplessly over the edge. Would no one even try to save the drowning man?

"Stop the boat!" exclaimed Hudson. He struck down the sail, and leaped overboard into the deep water. The Chinese man had sunk from sight, and the missionary was not sure where to find him. Diving repeatedly below the surface, he searched frantically for the man in the murky water.

"I must find him!" Hudson gasped as he came up for air. "He was not ready to believe in Jesus, so he isn't ready to die!" Shaking away the water that streamed into his eyes, Hudson saw the hulk of the large fishing boat approaching. *That net!* he thought. *The net would find him!*

"Hey!" he shouted, beckoning to the men on the fishing boat. "Come quickly and let down your net over this spot! There is a man drowning here!"

The Chinese fishermen stared at him. "It's not convenient," one answered lazily.

"Don't talk of *convenience*!" cried Hudson, horrified. "A man is drowning, I tell you!"

"We are busy fishing," another man told him with a scowl. "We cannot come, we would lose a lot of time!"

"Never mind your fishing!" Hudson called desperately. "I will give you more money than many days' fishing would bring. Only come quickly!"

"How much money will you give us?" a fisherman asked, interested at last.

"I will give you five dollars," promised Hudson, knowing that the fishermen seldom saw such a large sum in those days. "Only come, before it is too late!"

"We won't do it for that," responded the fishermen. "Give us twenty dollars, and we will drag with our net."

"I don't have that much!" cried Hudson in agony. "I only have about fourteen dollars, but I will give you *all* of it! Please come at once!"

Finally the fishermen paddled their boat over, and the net was let down. In less than a minute the body of the missing man was brought up and dropped upon the deck of the hong-boat. He lay very still. Was it too late?

"Give us our money!" "Pay us what you promised!" clamored the fishermen, but Hudson knelt first over the body of the man he had tried to save. Vainly he tried to resuscitate the drowned man, but it was no use. Life had already fled.

Rising to his feet, the dripping wet missionary looked sternly at the fishermen. "Here is your money," he said. His voice was sad. "I will pay you as I promised. But if only you had come at once when I called! This man's life could probably have been saved."

After changing into dry clothes, the weary missionary lay shivering with the strain and shock of what he had just seen. *Those fishermen were guilty of a man's death,* he thought. *All because they were too busy fishing! They would not leave their fishing even to save a life!*

In the stillness, a new thought came to Hudson Taylor. Those Chinese fishermen were cruel and heartless. But how many Christians are no better? How many Christians have no time to go tell others about Jesus? They will not try to save dying souls, because they are too busy with their own lives... too busy fishing!

Hudson bowed his head. "Lord, help me," he prayed. "Help me to bring the Gospel to as many Chinese people as I can, since You have called me to this country. I pray that You will speak to other Christians everywhere, that they must obey Your command to bring the Gospel to all!"

Historical Note:

James Hudson Taylor was born in England in 1832. His parents, before his birth, promised the Lord that their son should be a missionary for China. As a young man, Hudson studied to be a doctor, then sailed to China at the age of 21. For the next fifty years he was active in mission work, mostly in China.

Hudson Taylor has been called "the father of modern missions". Full of the Holy Spirit and faith, he was a man of great self-denial and dedication. Hundreds of thousands of Chinese people found the Lord through his witness. Hudson Taylor was the founder of the China Inland Mission.

9

MAMMA LILLIAN

"Lady, you must take this baby," ordered the old Egyptian woman. "I don't want it. She's only a girl!"

Lillian, the missionary, stared at the old woman in dismay. Answering an urgent cry for help, she had come tonight to this poor hut just in time to watch a young Egyptian mother die, leaving her tiny half-starved baby. The baby's tiny body was not much more than a skeleton already. If her mother was dead and her relatives didn't want her, Lillian was afraid that the baby had no chance to live.

Lillian lived in a small mission house with several other Christians, and there was not much room for a stray baby. But what other choice did she have? The child could not be left to die!

"Lord, what shall I do?" the young missionary prayed as she walked homeward down the dirt road, carrying the poor thin baby. And all at once the answer came:

This is why I have called you to Egypt. You must start a Christian orphanage for children of Egypt who have no homes!

Lillian obeyed the Lord's direction. A few days later she rented a house with some of the last money she had brought with her from America. With Fareida, the tiny Egyptian baby, she moved into the house. Soon the word spread about this Christian lady, who was kind enough to take the children other people didn't want and more children came to the little orphanage.

Many times Lillian wondered where she would find money to buy food for all her children. She was not allowed to get a job because she was not an Egyptian. There was no mission board giving support to her orphan's home. But Lillian knew that the Lord would provide, and somehow He always did! One morning when there was no food left in the house, a young boy came to her door to deliver a message.

"Is this the place where they take children with no homes?" he asked curiously after he had handed the note to Lillian.

"Yes, it is," the missionary answered.

"You will need a lot of money, won't you?" the boy observed.

Lillian smiled. "I suppose we will," she told the boy. "But God knows all about it, and He will provide for all our needs."

The boy stared at her with wonder in his dark face. Suddenly reaching into his own pocket, he put something in Lillian's hand. Then he turned and ran down the street.

The missionary looked at the small pile of coins in her hand and counted seven Egyptian piasters, which would make about thirty-five cents. One piaster was enough to buy a loaf of bread, and seven would feed her little family for a few days. "Thank You, Lord!" Lillian whispered.

Soon the house became too small for Lillian's growing family, and the Lord provided money to buy a small piece of land beside the Nile River.

"We will have to make our own bricks," Lillian told the children, and so they did. The Egyptian recipe for homemade bricks was probably still the same as it had been when the Israelites were slaves in Egypt! All the children who were old enough helped "Mamma Lillian" dig up piles of dirt, mix it with chopped straw and add water from the river to make mud. After stomping in the mud until it was mixed thoroughly, they would pack it into wooden molds and carry them to be baked hard in a brick kiln nearby.

After months of hard work, the new brick orphanage was finished! How the children rejoiced as they thanked God for providing a comfortable new home.

Day after day, "Mamma Lillian" would ride around the countryside on her donkey, finding children in need. The Egyptians in the villages knew her well and even though they were poor, they usually had something to share with her to help feed and clothe the orphans.

Even when Lillian was away, the work of the orphanage went on. The big girls cooked and took care of the little children while the boys made chairs to sell in town.

In those days the country of Egypt was trying to gain its independence from England. One Spring, fighting broke out in the town where Lillian lived with her children. Gunfire crackled all around, and many houses were burning. "Kill the Englishmen!" "Kill the Christians!" men shouted, and the sounds of battle were dangerously near.

Mamma Lillian calmly gathered her older children together. "Each one of you must carry two of the babies," she told them, "and we will go hide in the brick kiln!" Under cover of darkness, the nearly one hundred children slipped silently from their home and hurried to the empty brick factory. Lillian, her own arms full of babies, followed last. Inside the brick kiln, she counted her children.

"Oh, no!" she gasped. "Two are missing— two of the babies! I must go back to the house and get them."

"Don't, Mamma Lillian," whimpered the older girls. "Don't go out there! You will be killed!"

But the missionary was determined. "I must save the babies," she whispered. "Pray for me that God will keep me safe!" And she was off, sometimes running and sometimes crawling along the path to the orphanage.

"Stop!" came a sudden shout in the darkness.

"Who's that?" Shots rang out! *They are after me,* Lillian thought fearfully. Dropping to the ground, she rolled into a ditch and lay still. Running feet pounded along the path as soldiers searched for the unknown figure they had seen. Suddenly Lillian realized that she was not alone in the ditch! Close beside her lay the crumpled form of a dead soldier.

Nearer and nearer came the footsteps of the searchers, and Lillian prayed silently. All at once a heavy boot trampled her shoulder as a soldier stepped right on her in the darkness! Lillian held her breath. But the man seemed to think he had only stepped on the dead soldier, for he kept right on going!

Lying perfectly still, Lillian waited until the sound of boots and voices faded in the distance. Then, cautiously hugging the ground, she continued on. Quickly finding the two whimpering toddlers in their bedroom, she set out once more for the brick oven.

"Oh, Mamma Lillian! You're back— thank God!" her older children cried out softly as the missionary sat down to rest on the earthen floor of the kiln

"Yes, God kept me safe as you prayed," the tired Lillian responded. "He is faithful."

Historical Note:

"Mamma Lillian" in this story was Lillian Trasher, an American missionary to Egypt in the early part of the 20th century. Her night-time escape to the brick kiln happened in 1919. Later that year Lillian had to leave Egypt, but she soon returned when the fighting was over, and the work of the orphanage went on.

In all, more than eight thousand children found a home at Lillian's orphanage, where they were fed and clothed and taught to read the Bible. It is reported that every one of those 8,000 grew up to be good men and women.

10

THE SHOTGUN THAT
WOULDN'T FIRE

Twelve teenage boys sat in a circle around the glowing fire. "Here comes Brother Kwan!" Miguel whispered eagerly to his friend Francisco.

Tall, thin missionary John Beekman, whom the Indians called "Kwan", swung nimbly down the ladder from his house. "Good morning, brothers!" he greeted the boys. "The sun will soon be up, and then you will need to go to your work in the corn-fields. What Scripture have you chosen for your messages this Sunday?"

Miguel and his friends were Christian believers, boys from the Chol Indian tribe in Mexico. Very few older men in the tribe were willing to help the missionary, so John Beekman depended on these teenage boys to help him carry the Gospel. The preacher boys walked to faraway villages on weekends, telling other Indians about Jesus.

"Say, Brother Kwan, listen to what happened to Bernabel last Sunday," Marcial reported. A wiry youth of sixteen, with thick black hair, Marcial's black eyes flashed with excitement as he continued. "We were just coming down the trail toward the village of La Gloria, where we had been invited to preach. Suddenly a shotgun boomed and pellets splattered the bushes all around us! Several men jumped out from behind a boulder, waving guns and machetes. 'Liars!' they shouted. 'Thieves! Get out of here or we will kill you!' We could see that they were drunk, so we didn't stop to argue. We scrambled through the brush and ran! At the edge of the jungle, Bernabel tripped over a root and fell flat on his face. Just as he dropped, a volley of bullets whistled through the air at the very place where he would have been if he had not fallen!"

Stocky, dark-skinned Bernabel grinned and spoke up, "God took care of me, just like the Bible says. All things work together for good to those who love the Lord, Brother Kwan!"

After John and the preacher boys had settled on a passage from the Bible, they discussed its meaning and how it could be illustrated with stories and questions for the people they would be teaching. When the missionary asked for a volunteer to practice giving the sermon, Miguel rose to his feet. Stepping back a little way from the group, the seventeen-year-old boy read aloud the Scripture that had been chosen. Then he began to preach about what the verses meant.

When Miguel finished, John asked, "Brothers, how can he improve?"

"He should look straight at the people," Bernabel replied. "Even when he reads the Bible verses, he can look up sometimes."

Francisco added, "He should speak louder so that people in the back row can hear."

"And he shouldn't scratch his ear while he preaches," Marcial added with a chuckle. "People might think he has a bug there."

"I'll try to remember," Miguel smiled, coming back to his seat in the circle.

"Now, brothers," said the missionary, "where do you think the Spirit of God is leading you to go this weekend?"

"I'll go to the village of Tumbala," one boy spoke up. "And I will go with you there," another volunteered.

Miguel had been thinking all that week about the village of San Pedro. "That's where I want to go," he told John Beekman. "I will be his partner," Francisco added.

"Brothers, there are bitter enemies of the Gospel in that village!" the missionary warned.

The boys refused to be frightened. "We *must* tell them about Jesus," Francisco said boldly, his eyes flashing. "If we die, we will go to heaven that much sooner!"

I'm glad Francisco is going with me, Miguel thought as the boys left the meeting. Francisco had always shown great courage in facing persecution on their preaching trips. Once Miguel had seen a man stick the point of his machete under Francisco's chin, threatening to cut his throat. Francisco hadn't even flinched as he kept on talking about Jesus, and soon his enemy had backed away!

On Friday, the white missionary gave his young preachers their equipment: precious copies of the parts of the Bible which had been translated into the Chol language, and medical kits which the boys could use to help sick people along the way. Each boy also carried a little bag of Indian corn balls to eat on the trip.

Chol Indian country in Southern Mexico is some of the wildest in the world. Swift rivers run through the bottoms of great gorges that split steep mountain ranges, and there is jungle everywhere. The jungle is so thick that if you step off the trail, you can hardly see three feet on either side! Monkeys, jaguars, and poisonous snakes abound. The Chol Indians work hard to clear small patches of jungle land, where they plant corn to eat.

Narrow trails connected the villages where the Chols lived, surrounded by their tiny cornfields. There was a pathetic sameness about the villages where people were not Christians. Dirty children in tattered clothing peered out of the smoky one-room huts. Their fathers often lay on the ground in a drunken sleep. Pigs ran everywhere, into the huts and out again, rooting through the mud and garbage. Bugs of all kinds crawled or flew into the huts, causing dozens of diseases. Indian fathers worked for the Mexican coffee ranchers, then spent most of their money at the ranch store to get drunk. If there was any money left, it usually went to the witch doctor!

"I remember when I was sick a few years ago," Francisco told Miguel now as the two boys tramped along the trail together. "My father called the witch doctor, and he came with a bowl full of ants' eggs he had dug from an anthill. He chanted a weird song as he cooked the ants' eggs over our fire. When they were hot, he plastered them all over my face and neck, but they didn't do a bit of good! Next he told my father to kill a chicken, and he painted the blood all over my body. When that didn't work, he said we had to kill a pig. He painted me with the pig's blood, but I only felt worse! So the witch doctor looked very sober, and shook his head. He whispered to my father: 'Your neighbors have stolen the boy's spirit. If you kill one of them tonight, your son will get well!'"

"Fortunately, my father decided to call the missionary instead. Brother Kwan gave me a shot of some medicine, and in a few days, I was well again. Now my whole family believes in Jesus."

Miguel and Francisco walked all day Friday and camped that night along the trail. It was Saturday when they arrived in San Pedro, and soon a large crowd of Indians gathered to hear the boys. Hope was written all over their faces as Miguel spoke to them about God's love.

But there were others in the village who didn't like what was happening! Drums began a low, threatening rumble somewhere on the edge of the little town. A Mexican rancher strolled up the unpaved street and watched with a scowl. "Let's get them!" he snarled to a friend. "These preachers will cause our Indians to follow foreign ways and quit buying our whiskey!"

Gun in hand, the rancher shoved through the group of men and women. "Get back to your work, you lazy Indian bums," he growled. "Don't you know the foreign missionaries just want to kill you all and put you up for canned meat? And I'll show you how we take care of troublemakers like these two!"

Leveling his shotgun until it pointed at Miguel's stomach, he pulled the trigger. Everything happened so fast, Miguel didn't even have time to be frightened. The gun came up, the trigger made a small nasty click in the sudden silence, and that was all! The gun did not fire. The rancher's mouth dropped open. He stared at his gun in surprise. Then he lifted it up for a closer look, shook it, and muttered a curse.

"Jesus died for you, too, Señor," came Francisco's steady voice. "Won't you listen to what we..."

"No!" yelled the rancher. Pointing the shotgun at Francisco, he pulled the trigger again!

Once more, nothing happened. A quiet murmur of nervous laughter began here and there in the crowd, then died down as the rancher glared furiously at those who dared to mock him.

"Tie them up and bring them along!" he ordered four of his men. The men tied Francisco and Miguel, who did not resist as they were dragged away to the ranch house. They prayed for God's protection as the rancher's men locked them up in a small, dirty room. Like Paul and Silas, they kept up their courage through the night by singing and praying.

On Sunday morning, the rancher took Miguel and Francisco in a canoe downriver to the town of Salto. He marched them to the town plaza and handed an accusation to the judge. "These fellows were disturbing the peace in San Pedro," he told the judge. "They burned a sacred idol and started a riot!"

A crowd quickly gathered to hear what would happen next. "Did you destroy this idol?" the judge asked the Christians.

"No," Francisco replied calmly. "He is lying to you. We were only telling our poor Chol brothers about the true and living God! I used to dress in rags," the boy continued. "I didn't know how to read or write. What money I had, I wasted on whiskey. That's how the Chols of San Pedro still live, and I want to help them find what I found! Now I have good clothes and shoes to wear. I can read and write. But most of all, I have peace in my heart! The Word of God has made me different."

"We didn't come to make trouble, but to tell others of the Gospel that can change them, too," Miguel added. "If you want to hear the message we are bringing, let me read a little for you."

The judge nodded, ignoring the rancher's scowl. Miguel quickly turned to the Ten Commandments and read them aloud. Then he looked at Francisco and the two boys began singing together a simple chorus about the joy of the Lord.

When they finished, the judge looked hard at the shifty-eyed rancher. "These boys have broken no laws," he said sternly. "I am letting them go. Be sure you never bother me with such foolish accusations again!"

Miguel and Francisco left the plaza in triumph and visited the town jail. There they preached and sang for the prisoners, guards and many towns-people who were lounging around. Then they started the long walk home. It was Tuesday before they reached their own village, but they sang as they came up the trail toward John Beekman's house.

"God is powerful!" Miguel shouted happily as they met the missionary. "He takes care of us while we preach His Word!"

Historical Note:

Miguel and Francisco's miraculous escape happened in Mexico in the early 1960's. John Beekman and his wife Elaine were pioneer missionaries and Bible translators among the Chol tribe.

John had had a weak heart ever since boyhood, but he felt a definite call to the mission field. His doctor told John that he probably wouldn't live past the age of forty years. "But if I were you," said the doctor, "I would rather give a few years of my life to those who have never heard the Gospel than more years to those who have already heard." "Thanks a lot, Doctor! That is just what I wanted to hear!" John responded.

Before John Beekman died, he was able to see a strong church of about 9,000 Christians, in 70 congregations, among the Chol Indians.

11

JIM ELLIOT

AND THE AUCA INDIANS

Jim Elliot was a boy who loved Jesus. One day a friend of his parents asked him if he was going to be a preacher when he grew up. "I don't know," Jim replied. "But I would like to tell someone about Jesus, that never heard of Him before!" And that is just what happened.

When Jim grew up, he and his wife Betty were missionaries to the Indians in South America. They met a missionary from Ecuador, who told them about the needs of the Indians in that country. There were several different tribes of Indians living in the jungle. Some of them were being taught by missionaries already. Others had never heard of Jesus. One of these tribes was a wild and savage people called Aucas!

The Aucas were great hunters in the jungle. They hunted wild pigs, monkeys, and jaguars with their spears and bows and arrows. Auca Indians always went barefoot, and they could recognize another person's footprint like we recognize the faces of our friends! But the Aucas didn't know about Jesus.

The lives of the Aucas were dark and sad and full of fear. They had many cruel customs. If they saw anyone in the jungle who was not of their tribe, they would sneak up and kill them with their spears. They also speared each other, killing their own friends and relatives during the slightest quarrel. When a man killed another man, the family of the dead man would hunt for the killer and spear him too. Often parents killed their own children, just because they were tired of taking care of them. Everyone was always afraid of being suddenly killed! That is how people live, when they don't know anything about Jesus or God's laws or how to be kind.

Jim and Betty Elliot and their friends felt sorry for the Auca Indians. They wanted to help them learn about Jesus, so they could be free from their darkness and fear. But how could they get into the Auca's village without being killed?

Several missionary families built themselves houses in the jungle. They lived with the friendly tribe of Quichua Indians, across the river from the Aucas. They learned the Indian language, and preached to them about Jesus. Many of the

Quichua Indians became Christians. But Jim could not forget about the poor sad Auca Indians. He wanted to tell them about Jesus, too!

There was one Auca girl who lived with the friendly Quichua Indians. Her name was Dayuma, and she had run away from the Aucas several years before when someone was trying to kill her. Now the missionaries talked with her, to learn the Auca language.

The missionaries decided to try flying their little plane over the Auca village, and dropping gifts to the Indians. They hoped that this would be a way to make friends with the Aucas! They would put the presents in a bucket at the end of a strong fishing line, and lower it down from the open door of the plane. Nate Saint, the pilot, experimented until he found a way to release the bucket from the line and set it on the ground.

The first gift was a shiny aluminum kettle with a lid. Inside they put twenty brightly colored buttons, not for the Indian's clothes, because the Auca Indians didn't wear any clothes! But Jim thought the Indians might like to string the buttons and use them for decorations.

The first time Nate and Jim flew over the Auca village, the people were all frightened and hid inside their houses. A brisk wind buffeted the small plane as Nate tried to hold it steady over the group of thatched houses. Cautiously Jim reeled out the line. The kettle almost got caught in the trees, and he pulled it back a little... then set it down gently right in front of the biggest house!

The second time they let down the bucket with

a shiny long knife called a machete. It was wrapped in canvas so no one would get hurt, and tied with pretty ribbons. This time Jim and his friends brought the gifts to another house, so the Aucas would not get jealous of each other. And this time when the Indians heard the plane coming over, they ran out of their houses! They watched excitedly as the gift was lowered from the plane. A gust of wind blew the gift bucket toward the river, and splash! It dropped in. Then, quick as a wink, there was another splash! as an Indian dived in for the treasure. They soon found it, and stood around talking happily. Jim saw a sight that thrilled him: an old man waving with his arms as if to say, "Come down!" As the plane turned and flew away, Jim prayed: *Lord, send me to the Aucas!*

Every week after that, the missionaries made another flight to drop gifts to the Auca Indians. They gave them shirts, knives, and plastic cups, candy and a flashlight. They began to fly lower and lower above the Auca village, and would lean out the door of the plane to shout at the Indians: "We are your friends! We would like to visit you!"

On the sixth flight, after the Aucas had taken the gift bucket, they held onto the line for a few minutes. When they let it go, it came up with a present for the missionaries: a headband woven of feathers! The next time they sent a basket back up on the line. In the basket was a beautiful tame parrot, with a banana for the parrot to eat! Jim and his friends praised the Lord. It seemed like the Aucas were becoming friendly.

Other people said, "You fellows are crazy to waste all that good stuff on the Aucas. They will be just as mean as before." But the missionaries kept praying that God would make the Auca Indians friendly, so that they could tell them about Jesus.

After about two months of flying over the Auca village with gifts, the missionaries decided it was time to land on a little beach beside the river, close to where the Aucas lived. They would build themselves a tree house to live in, and try to talk to the Aucas.

There were five men altogether: Jim, Nate, and three others named Pete, Roger, and Ed. They prayed and talked with their wives for a long time before they made the decision to move into the Auca's country. All of them knew very well that it was dangerous. But they loved God and knew that they belonged to Him. They were not afraid to die and go to heaven.

So they landed their plane beside the river and built a house in a tall tree. Some of the men flew over the Auca village again, calling: "Come down to the river! We want to visit you there!" Then they camped and waited.

On the third day, the men were sitting in their camp, when suddenly they heard a shout from across the river! Their hearts jumped as they turned to look. Three Aucas were stepping out of the woods: a man and two women. Calling out, "Welcome! Welcome!" in the Auca language, Jim waded across to meet them. He took their hands and helped them back across to the missionaries' camp. The five missionaries tried hard to show the Aucas that they wanted to be friends. They gave them food and gifts, and smiled and talked. They soon nicknamed the Auca man "George", and when "George" asked for a ride in the plane, they were happy to give him one! They flew the plane low over the Auca village once more, and George laughed with delight as he recognized his home. He leaned out to wave and yell at the other Aucas. When the plane landed back at camp, the five missionaries gave thanks to God out loud, looking up toward the sky so that the three Aucas could see what they were doing.

That night the three Aucas returned to their village. They did not invite the missionaries to come with them, so Jim and his friends stayed at their camp. That was on Friday. On Sunday, Nate called his wife on the radio to say that a big group of Auca men were coming. "Just in time for a church service!" he told her excitedly. "This is the big day! I'll call you back this afternoon and let you know what happens!"

So the missionaries' wives waited eagerly that afternoon. They were hoping to find out if the men had been able to visit the Auca's village. But the afternoon passed, and the men did not call as they had promised. Night came on and the women began to worry. What could have happened? Were the missionaries safe? The next day more men took another plane and flew over the camp. They brought back sad news: Jim and Nate and their friends were all dead. The Auca Indians had killed them with their spears!

The five missionaries had guns with them in their camp, but they did not use them to fight the Indians. When the Auca men came toward them with their spears, they did not shoot back with their guns. They knew that if they would shoot the Indians, they could probably save their own lives. But then they would never be able to teach the Aucas about Jesus! So they chose to let themselves be killed, and let the Aucas have another chance to become Christians.

The Aucas always remembered those five strange white men who had been so kind to them and had not tried to kill them. And so a year later when more missionaries tried again to speak to the Aucas about Jesus, they were ready to listen. Several of the men who had helped to kill Jim and his friends with their spears now became Christians. One of them gave his testimony at a meeting. He counted on his fingers and said, "I have killed twelve people with my spear! But I did that when my heart was black. Now Jesus' blood has washed my heart clean, so I don't live like that anymore." God's love had changed his life!

Historical Note:

The death of these five brave missionaries happened on January 8, 1956. Jim Elliot, Nate Saint, Roger Youderian, Ed McCully, and Pete Fleming did much for the Kingdom of God. Not only did the Aucas learn about Jesus' forgiveness and love, but many other people all over the world decided to serve the Lord too after they heard the story.

12

THE MIRACLE FROM THE

MEADOW

"Just look at that meadow, full of flowers!" Margaret exclaimed in German.

"Yes, they are beautiful," Amy Bontrager replied in the same language. "Austria is a lovely country, with all these rolling hills and mountains."

"I'd like to stop and pick some," the German lady chattered on. "Do you think we could? They would make such a beautiful Fall bouquet!"

"Should we?" Amy murmured in English to her husband David.

"I suppose we could stop for a little," David Bontrager answered. "No one will mind if Margaret picks a few wild flowers out of a field, but we can't stay long if we are going to cross the Romanian border before night."

He brought the car to a stop beside the country road and the two women got out. While Amy and their German friend Margaret moved happily through the field of flowers, David sat idly in the driver's seat of the rented car. Like speedy birds, his thoughts were soon far away... far across the ocean, to his home in Indiana! *We are a long way from home,* David mused.

For many years David Bontrager, an American minister, had felt a special concern for persecuted Christians in the Communist nations of Europe. *If only there was something we Christians in America could do to help them!* he had thought. And now God had shown him a way. Working together with a Christian mission in West Germany, David had begun taking trips into the Communist countries of Hungary, Romania, and Russia. As an American tourist, it was not too difficult for him to get in. Once he entered a country, he did all he could to encourage the Christians there. Often, he preached for them. Usually his luggage contained many Bibles, tracts, and other items that were forbidden or hard to find behind the Iron Curtain. On this trip, he had a suitcase loaded with gifts which would be helpful to poor Christian families in Romania.

The sound of voices outside the car brought David back to the present.

"Look at my flowers!" Margaret was crying out happily in German. And Amy was laughing, "She sure picked a big bunch. What kind of flowers are they, I wonder?"

"*I* sure don't know," David grinned, eyeing the fluffy-topped stalks. "They look sort of like dandelions back home in the Spring, when they go to seed. If we don't look out, they'll spread fuzz all over in the car!"

"Put them in the trunk," Amy advised Margaret. "Lay them on top of the suitcases and they should be all right."

Little did David know, as he carefully lowered the lid of the trunk over the strange bouquet, how God would soon be using these dried flowers to protect the three missionaries from danger!

The travellers crossed the border between Austria and Hungary with no trouble, and spent most of that day driving through Hungary. The Romanian border, though, was the danger spot.

As they drove through the small Hungarian village where they planned to cross the border into Romania, David and Amy felt rather tense and anxious. "No matter how many times we do this, it always scares me," David murmured to his wife. "We are driving right into the hands of the Communists, into a country where our brethren in Christ are persecuted. The guards usually seem very polite to tourists, but if they knew about everything we have in our suitcases..." he left the sentence unfinished.

"We are doing the Lord's work, and we are in His hands," Amy encouraged quietly. "Let's keep praying! That's the best thing we can do."

"There's the place!" Margaret said softly in

German. Ahead of the travelers, a stout barrier blocked the street. Beside it stood a grim guardhouse with a uniformed man in the doorway and another guard visible through a small window. Breathing one last quick prayer, David drove slowly up to the station and stopped.

The border guard who strolled over to David's window did not smile. Hard-faced and stern, he wore the uniform of the Romanian military police. "How many?" he asked brusquely.

"Just the three of us," David replied. As he handed over their passports, he tried not to look at the ominous bulge of the officer's gun.

The guard examined the three passports while the travelers waited quietly. "What is your purpose in coming to Romania?" he questioned. "We are on our way to visit friends in Romania," David answered, as pleasantly as he could.

"Do you have anything to declare?" was the next question.

"Well, we have money and each of us has a watch and here is my camera," David began. "No drugs, no liquor?" the guard asked. David shook his head, "No!"

"Hmmm," grunted the guard. He bent and peered in the window of the back seat. "Everybody get out!" he snapped. Soon both guards were searching the inside of the car, while David, Amy, and Margaret stood beside it trying not to look worried.

"Now, the trunk," the first guard told David at last. With the keys in his hand, David opened the trunk of the car.

"Open one of those suitcases," the guard ordered.

"Certainly," David answered politely. *Maybe he will only look inside one and not the rest!* he thought hopefully. Two suitcases lay side by side in the trunk and David reached for the one which held only the Bontrager's clothing and personal things. The guard leaned close to look as David lifted the lid. "No, not this one!" he barked suddenly. "I want to see inside that suitcase!" Gesturing with one heavy hand, he pointed to the other suitcase. Margaret's dried bouquet lay on top, but inside... David's heart sank. Inside that suitcase were the dangerous items: Christian literature and gifts for the struggling Christian brothers and sisters of Romania! What would this officer do when he found the forbidden things?

"Open *that* suitcase!" the guard repeated and there was nothing to do but obey. Nervously, David dropped the lid of the suitcase he had already opened.

Whoosh! A puff of wind, created by the falling lid, swept through the dry bouquet where it decorated the top of the other suitcase. Suddenly the air was full of flying fluff and downy seeds as the bouquet flew apart, right into the face of the officer!

"Pffui!" spluttered the astonished guard, blinking and waving both hands in front of his face. "I... uh... AH-CHOO! Ah-choo!" he sneezed violently, scattering more seeds in all directions.

"My flowers!" gasped Margaret, looking like she wasn't sure whether to laugh or cry.

David wanted to laugh, but of course he did not dare. "I'm so sorry, sir," he apologized. "You must be allergic to weeds like this. Shall I ..."

"No, no!" the guard answered impatiently, turning away to blow his nose. "I've seen quite enough. Just close your trunk and you may go!"

As the travelers drove through Romania, they enjoyed a good laugh over their narrow escape. "Too bad about your bouquet, Margaret," David chuckled. "I surely didn't mean to scatter it apart! But the Lord used it to get us safely through. Of all the ways God has protected us on our trips, I think this was the funniest!"

Historical Note:
This incident happened during the 1970's on one of David Bontrager's trips to Romania. In those days, Hungary, Romania, and Russia were Communist dictatorships where Christians lived lives of poverty and suffering.

The Friedenstimme Mission in Germany was made up of Christians who had escaped from these Communist countries. David Bontrager made many trips to Europe to work with the Friedenstimme mission. He carried many Bibles and tracts into the countries where Christians were not free. On the trip mentioned in this story he was also carrying many small items such as watches which the Christians in Romania could sell for money to live on.

In 1971, David Bontrager started a mission organization, Jesus To the Iron Curtain. This mission is still operating today, but its name has been changed to Christian Mission Charities.

David Bontrager died in 1989.

13

SHE CHANGED HER MIND

"I will never be a missionary! Never, never!" cried Ida Scudder. "I'm going to stay in America always, where it's clean and comfortable. I will have a good job and make plenty of money. I'm never going back to India!"

Ida's parents were missionaries in India. So was her grandfather. Six of her uncles and many of her cousins had also chosen to work for the Lord among the poor people of India. But not Ida! She hated the poverty of India, the heat and dirt and the flies. She couldn't stand to see the beggars and hear about children starving to death.

Now that Ida had been sent to school in America, she was determined that she would never return to India! But God had other plans for Ida.

Just before she was to graduate from school, an urgent message arrived from her father. "Your mother is seriously ill! Come at once."

"Yes, I must go to her," Ida decided. "But as soon as Mother is well again, I'm leaving! I will never stay in India."

So Ida boarded a ship for India, and in a few days, she was back at the mission— amid the dust and heat and poverty she remembered. Obediently she cared for her mother and helped her father with the work of the mission. But when her mother grew stronger, Ida's thoughts turned back to her comfortable life and friends in America.

"I'll be coming home again soon," Ida wrote one night in a letter to one of her friends. Sitting at her desk, Ida looked disdainfully at the cloud of bugs that were trying to get through the screen to her lamp. *Soon I'll be back in America, where there aren't so many bugs,* she thought.

Suddenly Ida heard soft footsteps on the verandah outside her window. At her door, the footsteps stopped, and she heard someone cough, as Hindus do instead of knocking.

Picking up her lamp, Ida went to the door and opened it. A young Hindu man stood before her, with an anxious look on his face.

"Lady, will you please come to help my wife?" he begged. "She is dying and needs a doctor!" "I'm sorry," Ida told the man. "I'm not the doctor, my father is. I will take you to him at once!" The young man drew back, shocked.

"No!" he cried. "We are high-born Hindus, and no man has ever looked upon my wife's face. I want *you* to come! My wife would rather die than have a man doctor see her."

"But I don't know anything about medicine," said Ida. "I wouldn't be able to help her."

"Then she must die," said the young Hindu in despair and was gone into the night before Ida could answer.

Sadly, Ida returned to her letter-writing, but somehow she could think of nothing to say. As she sat staring at the paper, the sound of footsteps came again on the verandah!

Ida jumped up and went to the screen door, hoping that the Hindu had returned. But there stood another man, a well-dressed Mohammedan, bowing politely before her.

"May Allah give you peace, Madam," he said. "My wife is very ill and I have come to ask you to visit her. I heard that you are a new doctor from America."

Another one! Ida's heart sank.

"I'm not a doctor, my *father* is the doctor!" she said earnestly. "I will call him, and if you want me to, I will come along and help."

"No, Madam, that will be impossible," the Mohammedan replied haughtily. "My religion forbids women to be seen by men outside their own family. I will not bring to her a doctor who is a man!"

Ida ran to her room and closed the door. *Oh, I wish I were far away from India, where the people are so stubborn and ignorant!* she thought. But as she was preparing to go to bed, there came a third knock on her door.

This time the man in the dark verandah was a

man Ida knew, the father of a child who came to the mission kindergarten. His wife was a pretty young girl, no older than Ida.

"Please, lady," the man stammered eagerly. "Will you come and bring medicine for my wife? She is burning with fever!"

"I am not a doctor," said Ida again. "I would not know what to do for her. Let me call my father!" But she knew, before he even opened his mouth, what the man would say. He would not let a man come near his wife. He wanted a woman!

"If you will not help her, she will die," the man moaned as he went down the steps and into the darkness.

Slowly Ida returned to her bed. But she could not sleep. How could this thing happen three times in one evening? Three knocks on the door and three calls for help. Was God calling her, like He called Samuel in the night?

If I were a doctor, Ida thought, *I could save the lives of many women and girls here in India. They need a woman doctor, to stop this needless suffering!*

Early the next morning, Ida sent a servant to find out about the three sick women whose husbands had come in the night.

"They all died," the servant said sadly when he returned. "All are dead."

"All dead!" Ida repeated slowly. Going back to her room, she knelt in prayer. *God has called me, and I must obey,* she decided. *I will study to be a doctor, and then I can work for the Lord here in India.*

With a light heart, Ida went to tell her parents of her decision. How pleased they would be!

Historical Note:

Ida became Dr. Ida Scudder, who worked for the rest of her life in India. She built several hospitals in the town of Vellore, which later became the greatest medical center in all of Asia. Dr. Ida Scudder taught the people of India, by her words and deeds, that God is love.

14

THE TIGER IS LOOSE!

"The tiger cannot possibly escape from the basket," said the sergeant.

"Are you sure?" Jack, the missionary pilot, stood beside his small plane. Pushing back his cap, he wiped a trail of sweat from his forehead and looked doubtfully at the huge wicker basket. Inside the basket, which had been made from reeds and strips of bark, crouched a fierce-looking spotted cat. The "tiger" was really an ocelot, a tawny South American panther.

"Oh, sí, Señor," the Peruvian soldier assured Jack. His white teeth flashed in his swarthy face as he grinned. "The tiger cat will be quite safe in your plane! My basket is very strong."

Jack was not enthusiastic about having a wild ocelot aboard the plane. It looked pretty mean!

He was flying alone on this trip with a cargo of supplies for different mission stations. *I'm already carrying four live chickens and two turtles in a box, Jack mused. This plane is turning into a Noah's Ark!* But Jack remembered the mission director's rule: "Always cooperate with the government people whenever possible. We are in their country by permission, to preach the Gospel. So be courteous!"

"Yes, I will take your tiger along and deliver her to your friend," Jack agreed. The two men loaded the big basket behind a back seat. The plane skimmed lightly over the river on its pontoons and rose into the air.

Jack was flying one of a small fleet of mission airplanes, which soared daily over the most savage, dangerous jungles of South America. Any mistake on his part could bring his plane crashing down to vanish in the trackless expanse of jungle, where death waited in many forms. Poisonous plants, deadly snakes, man-eating fish with razor-sharp teeth, and head-hunting Indians all lurked in the thick green rain forests.

Before airplanes came to the South American missions, the missionaries and Bible translators had needed to travel on foot through the treacherous jungle trails or by small boats on the rivers. A trip to the nearest town or doctor might take ten or twenty days of dangerous travel. But now, pilots like Jack took the same trip in an hour. This made things so much easier for the brave missionaries who were risking their lives to bring the Gospel to the Indians!

Jack whistled happily, thinking about this. His hands skilfully held the controls as he peered through the plexiglass windows of the cockpit. Three thousand feet below were the lush jungles of Northern Peru, with the strangely black waters of the Nanay river churning through them.

Suddenly a flurry of squawking noises erupted from the seat behind Jack. It sounded just like the noise the chickens had made on his father's farm, the time a fox had crept into their henhouse late at night! Whirling around in his seat, Jack saw that the ocelot had escaped. She was climbing over the seat, yellow eyes gleaming as she hungrily looked at the chickens!

Grabbing his canteen, Jack threw water at the big cat. Snarling, she slunk back to the luggage compartment. In just a few moments, though, she started over the seat again! Frantic, the chickens flopped their wings and fought to free their feet from the vines that tied them together. Jack hurled his empty canteen at the cat. He missed, and the ocelot pounced, landing in the seat beside the chickens. Snapping the weed-vines around their feet, the panicked chickens exploded in all directions! Their wings beat against the windows and in Jack's face as the ocelot stood up on her hind legs, sharp claws swinging for a drumstick! Feathers flew everywhere.

Jack forgot all about flying the airplane and began grabbing for chickens. But it was no use! The ocelot soon had a chicken trapped on the floor under Jack's seat, and he could hear its sharp teeth crunching on flesh and bones.

The plane was three thousand feet up in the air, and no help was near. What could Jack do? Would the ocelot be satisfied after her chicken dinner, and sleep for a while? Or would she decide to hunt for more meat?

Slash! One tawny foreleg, tipped with steely claws, shot out from under the seat toward Jack. For an instant the ocelot's claws hooked into the pilot's pants, then tore free. Jack's pounding heart seemed to be squeezing the breath from his lungs. The "tiger" was hunting *him*! With all his might, Jack kicked back at his enemy. She yowled a blood-curdling cry of rage that filled the small plane.

"Lord, what shall I do? Help me find a place to land!" Jack prayed desperately. Looking out the window, he spotted a small settlement by the river below. Jack rolled down the flaps of his plane and began to circle around for a landing. Kicking the cat with his heels every time she reached for his leg, he finally got the plane down to the water.

A crowd of dark-skinned men appeared as Jack taxied the plane up to the bank. "Help!" he shouted out the window. "I have a loose tiger cat in here!" A dozen men jumped onto the pontoons at the same time, all trying to see into the plane, which began to sink.

"No!" cried Jack. "Not all at once!" The men jumped off again and their leader sent for a coil of rope. Soon the angry ocelot had been lassoed and safely tied up. Sighing with relief, Jack thanked the Peruvians.

"Oh, it is nothing," the leader smilingly told Jack. "We are just so glad you landed here! One of my men had a heart attack this morning and may die if we cannot get him to a hospital. Will you take him along to the city?"

"Of course, I will take him," Jack agreed.

So the Lord had a purpose in allowing the tiger cat to break loose, Jack mused as he helped lift the sick man into the airplane. *God used a snarling ocelot and a scared pilot to get His plane to the right place and save this man's life.*

Less than two hours later the sick man was safely in the hospital at Iquitos, the army officer had his ocelot, and Jack was on his way back to the mission at Yarinacocha.

Historical Note:
Jack, the pilot, was Jack McGuckin of Wycliffe Bible translator's Jungle Aviation Service. This incident happened in the 1960's, when Jack was on one of his first missionary flights in Peru.

15

SAVED IN THE NIGHT

"I'll race you to that tree!" eight-year-old Mark Kniss called to his older brother Paul. Standing up on the pedals, the missionary's two sons drove their bicycles as fast as they could along the dusty ox-cart trail.

Behind them came the rest of the caravan. Lloy Kniss, missionary to India, drove his old-fashioned Chevrolet slowly over the bumpy track. Beside him sat his wife Elizabeth and small daughter Esther, and in the back seat were two brown-skinned Bible women[1] and the wife of an Indian preacher.

Three Indian evangelists and an Indian cook rode their bicycles behind the car. Next came the ox carts, loaded with everything the mission group would need on a trip lasting two months! Tents, folding cots, buckets, books, medicines and food,

1. Common term in India for women who distributed Bibles and tracts

lanterns and tools were packed neatly into the wooden carts.

"I wish we had stayed in Bhotiyadihi awhile longer," Mark told his brother as they rested in the shade of the tree, waiting for the others to catch up. "That was one of the nicest camps we ever had. You know the big mango tree we slept under? I'd like to have hung a swing from that huge straight branch right above our tent."

"Yes, well, Father prayed about it," ten-year-old Paul answered. "He and the other preachers decided to leave today if the rain stopped and right after that they saw a big patch of blue sky. So tonight we will be in Panduka. Wonder what that camp will be like?"

The afternoon was bright and sunny as the missionary caravan rolled into the village of Panduka. Mark's father quickly secured permission from the village elders to camp under a cluster of big mango trees. Then he and the other mission men set up the tents and dug a shallow pit in the ground where they would build their fire.

A load of logs was carried from one of the oxcarts to the rough fire-pit. When the chilly evening came, many villagers would be attracted to the warmth and light of the missionaries' fire! Then the precious Gospel of Jesus could be shared with them in story and song.

When supper had been cooked and eaten by the fireside, dusk had fallen. Mark and his brother and sister stood watching as their father lighted the gas mantle lamp and hung it on a post. The clean, flaring white light pushed back all the dark shadows to the very edges of the camp, and made the children feel safe.

"This is the brightest place in the whole village," Paul observed to the others. "None of the Indian people have any lights like this. Pretty soon they will start coming to see ours!"

He was right. Down the narrow, winding streets of the village, people were coming. By twos and threes, and then in little groups, the villagers made their way toward the light and warmth of the missionaries' camp. The Christians welcomed them courteously, and then one of the Indian preachers led the group in a song.

By ten o'clock Mark was very tired. The meeting was over, but a few Indian men still lingered around the fire talking with the preachers as the women and children prepared for bed in their tents. Mark's eyes could not stay open as he tumbled sleepily onto the bag of crackling straw which served as a mattress for his cot. He could hear a murmur of men's voices outside the tent wall, and beyond them another sound, a moaning of leafy branches as the wind rose in the dark. *Sounds like a storm coming,* Mark thought as he fell asleep.

A few hours later, Mark suddenly jerked awake. Howling wind filled his ears, and the tent above him was flapping wildly. In the dim glow of a flashlight, he could see his father standing at one pole of the tent, leaning his weight against it. "What's wrong?" the startled boy cried out sleepily.

"It's a cyclone," his mother replied in a quiet

voice. "Don't wake Esther. God will keep us safe!"

Blinking, Mark looked around the tent. His mother was on her knees, holding the flashlight... and probably praying, too. His tall father stood immovable at the tent pole. Outside the storm raged on, but Mark could sense his parents' faith in the presence of God. Slowly his eyelids fluttered shut once more.

In the morning, the skies were so clear and blue that Mark wondered whether the storm in the night had been only a dream. But then he heard excited voices around the breakfast fire: "Hailstones?" "Yes, big hailstones! But not one fell on any of the mission tents!"

Dressing quickly, Mark ran out into the bright morning. All around him, the grown-ups were discussing the storm. "God must have been with us last night," one of the Indian preachers was declaring thankfully. "We came through that cyclone without damage to any of our tents!"

Suddenly a little group of women burst into the circle of missionaries, all chattering at once. "Your God saved you yesterday!" one cried out breathlessly. "We are from the village of Bhotiyadihi," another chimed in, "where your camp was until yesterday. And that big tree—" she stopped for breath, and another woman interrupted. "That big mango tree you camped under, it is gone! The storm brought it down right where your tent was." "Right on the very spot!" a fourth woman agreed. "If you had not moved yesterday, you would have been killed! Your God saved you. We have come to the market here in Panduka, but first we wanted to tell you about that tree!"

Mark stood at his father's elbow, listening. *That nice big tree!* he thought with a shiver. *And I wanted to stay there longer. But Father prayed, and God sent blue sky for a sign that we were to leave. It's good we obeyed God! He kept us safe again.*

Historical Note:

Lloy and Elizabeth Kniss were missionaries in Central India for sixteen years, from 1926 to 1942. This incident happened about 1935. Young Mark never forgot the night his family was saved from the storm. When he grew up he became a doctor and spent thirteen years with his wife as a missionary to India.

Mark Kniss is the author's uncle by marriage.

16

THE TALKING TORTILLA

"Here comes the plane!" shouted the children of the Shivalito mission school. They were Tila Indian children of Southern Mexico, and their sharp ears had picked up a distant whine of engines from the small Mission Aviation plane.

"It's coming over the mountain pass, Señorita Ruby!" a dark-skinned boy exclaimed. "And you said they are bringing something special today!"

Ruby Scott, the mission teacher, smiled as she put down the piece of chalk she had been using to write a math problem. "You may be dismissed, children," she told them. Her voice showed that she was excited, too! Today was the long-awaited day for the records to arrive.

Ruby and her co-worker Violet had worked with the Tila Indians for five years. First they had needed to learn the Tila language, so that they could "speak straight words", as the Indians said. Next they began translating the New Testament, one book at a time, into the language of the Tilas. Teaching school occupied much of their days, as they helped Tila children and adults learn to read and write.

Many older people, though, found reading too hard to learn. Also, many villages had never heard the Gospel at all, and there were not enough preachers to reach them. What could the missionaries use to share God's Word with *all* the Tila Indians? Today's airplane was bringing the answer!

The small airplane shuddered to a stop, and the pilot unloaded his special cargo: ten small phonographs and several boxes of records. The missionaries opened a box and as the Tilas of the village crowded around, Ruby placed a black record on the little turntable of one phonograph machine. "Here, Margarito," she beckoned the chief's son, "you crank this handle around until I tell you to stop." Always ready for some new excitement, the boy stepped forward and turned the crank.

Suddenly, the record started to play! The crowd of Tilas gasped fearfully and moved back. Children screamed and scrambled away as words poured from the new machine.

"It talks! The black tortilla talks!" they shrieked.

No Scripture class held by the missionary teachers had ever held the Tilas' attention so well!

The new records were pressed with Gospel messages in their own language: Scripture readings, songs, and stories.

"Mach'an yambu ba ch'ujbi lac tyaj laj cotyuntyel. Dios ma' ti yuc'onla yambu ti pejtyelel mulawil ba' mi lac tyaje laj cotyuntyel. Cojach ti Jesus!" said the record. "For there is no other name under heaven whereby we must be saved. Believe on the Name of Jesus!"

When the record stopped playing, Ruby held it up. A tall Indian reached out to touch it, then hesitated and jerked his hand back. What made that tortilla talk? Maybe it was dangerous! Mocking giggles sounded through the crowd. Getting up his courage, Venancio reached for the record again. When he had it safely in hand, others eagerly reached to touch it, too.

"Hey, it's hard," they called.

"And it has tiny lines that go all around it in circles," one man observed.

"Where are the words?"

"Why can't we see the words, like we see them on paper?"

"How do the words jump from this thing and speak with a voice like a person?"

The missionaries looked at one another helplessly, wondering how to explain. Before they could speak, the deep voice of an elderly Christian Tila rang out over the crowd. "God does it," he said. "There's nothing too hard for Him to do. God can make words jump from that black tortilla into the ears of people. He does it because He wants all to hear the true words."

The people were silent, and the missionary teachers could only nod their heads in agreement. Jorge, a respected elder who had asked God to turn his heart into the straight path, certainly had the answer!

"Now all the Tila people in faraway villages can crank the machine just like Margarito did, and hear God's Word speak," Violet told the people joyfully. "Pass the message around to all your friends that anyone who wishes may borrow a talking machine to play in their village."

In the days that followed, there were many requests to borrow the Gospel phonographs. All the Tilas wanted to hear the black tortillas that talked! The next mission airplane brought twenty more machines and records to go with them.

Domingo, a converted witch doctor who had never been able to learn to read, came to the missionaries. His face was covered with deep scars where he had been cut by a machete during a drunken fight fifteen years ago.

"I ran away from my village after that fight, and never returned," he told Ruby. "I have lived here ever since. But now Christ has turned my heart around. I want to go back and tell my friends about the Lord!"

So Domingo's name was written on the list of those who were borrowing a Gospel phonograph, and early the next morning he set off down the jungle trail. The trip to his old village took two days, and when he arrived, his friends greeted him happily. They laughed and talked, sharing memories of the "good old days".

But when they brought out a bottle of liquor, Domingo turned away. "See what I have here?" he said, opening the phonograph machine. He put on a record, and cranked the handle. His friends listened with awe as this strange black tortilla spoke in their language. It told of the true God who had made the sun and moon. The Tilas had always worshiped the sun and moon as gods!

"God isn't the sun up in the sky as we always thought," Domingo told his friends. "He is a Person, and He has grabbed my heart and turned it toward the straight trail."

Domingo's friends could not believe what they were hearing. "How can you, a witch doctor, turn your back on the spirits who chose you and gave you power?" one shouted. "Have you no pride?"

"Christ has *more* power than our old witchcraft," Domingo explained. "He is the Son of God, and He raised the dead and healed the blind. He has made my heart feel good, happier than I ever was before. He will make you happy, too, if you ask Him!"

Domingo's friends couldn't understand how he could stay so calm and quiet when they shouted at him. "You are turning into a woman," they mocked. "Get out of our village, before we show you how real men use machetes!"

Quickly, Domingo closed the phonograph and put the records back into his carrying bag. Sadly, he started down the trail. Weren't his friends going to hear the message that could save them? He *must* try one more time! Domingo stopped after he had taken a few steps and turned. "Please, my friends," he began, "Won't you listen..."

Furious, one of the men charged down the trail toward Domingo. His machete flashed as he swung it at the record player. Domingo's hand, holding the machine, was in the path of the sharp blade. CHOP! went the machete, and three of Domingo's fingers fell to the grass!

The angry man sheathed his machete and returned to his friends as Domingo hurried away. Tearing some cloth from his shirt, he tied up the hurt hand. Then he trudged wearily home.

Two days later, as he stood before Ruby, having his wounds bandaged, Domingo still had not given up.

"Those poor men," he told the missionary. "God's message just hasn't grabbed their hearts yet! I must go back and tell them again."

That night Ruby knelt in prayer, asking God to help her be as brave and faithful a missionary as poor Domingo, the former witch doctor.

Historical Note:

At the time of this writing, there are forty-eight churches scattered throughout the Tila Indian territory. Before Ruby and Violet left Mexico, they had translated the entire New Testament into Tila and also made a Tila Concordance and hymnbook.

Ruby Scott now lives among the Navajo Indians in Arizona. Her book, *Jungle Harvest*, tells the story of Domingo and other Tila Indians who became Christians.

Margarito, the chief's son in this story, became the first doctor among the Tilas.

17

MARTYRED AT MIDNIGHT

It was nearly midnight on a lonely, moonlit mountainside in Guatemala. A rocky footpath wound its way between scattered huts and corn patches, to the mission house and the church building on top of the ridge.

Behind the mission house, a cluster of pine trees sighed and whispered in the wind. Under their shadowy branches, the stealthy forms of several men lurked in the darkness. The faint glow of a cigarette showed eyes that smoldered with fanatical hatred.

"How much longer, Commandante?" whispered one of the terrorists in Spanish. He was uniformed in camouflage green and wore a gun strapped to his shoulders.

"Patience," the leader replied briefly. "We'll get those missionaries soon enough."

Inside the house, the missionary family slept. John Troyer, a tall young American minister; his wife Marie, who provided medical care for the local Indians from a makeshift clinic on her porch, and their five little children. The luminous pale green hands of the alarm clock beside Marie stood at ten minutes till midnight.

CRASH! BANG! The house shook, as heavy blows pounded upon the front door. "Out of the house! Get out with your hands up!" came a roar of angry voices from outside. Machetes slashed at the wooden door as the shouts of hatred slashed the air. "Get out immediately!"

Trembling, Marie crept from her bed and peered through the window curtain. John looked over her shoulder, and both gasped. The silvery bright moonlight showed three masked men on the porch, chopping at the door. In front of the porch were six or eight more men, the muzzles of their guns pointed toward the house. "Get dressed, Marie, quickly!" whispered John urgently. There was a hasty knock on the bedroom door, and Gary Miller, John's young coworker, burst in breathlessly. "What shall do, John?" he exclaimed softly.

"Is there any chance of slipping out the back door and going for help?" John wondered.

"No," Gary decided. "These men surely have our house surrounded! Let's pray." The three young missionaries dropped to their knees at the side of the bed.

"Oh, Father!" Gary cried out softly. "Please

keep us safe if it is your will. Forgive any sin in our lives..."

Crash! A gunshot exploded, splintering open the front door.

"Get out!" came the shouted command once more. "No one will be killed, we promise. Only come out, with your hands up!"

The missionaries looked at each other. There was no escape. John took Marie's hand. "Let's get the children," he said. "It's cold outside, so wrap a blanket around each of them."

Carrying their sleeping twin babies, the young parents led the other children into the dark living room. *If only I could wake up and find this was all a bad dream!* Marie thought. But she knew it was all too real.

"I'll go out first," Gary volunteered. Picking up four-year-old Marilyn, he stepped through the open doorway. Immediately he was surrounded by the terrorists, pointing their machine guns at him from every side. "¡Manos arriba!" "Hands up!" they commanded.

Gary wrapped Marilyn's arms around his neck, so he could hold his hands in the air as the men searched him for weapons.

Holding one baby, Marie took her oldest son's hand and came through the door. Shivering, she pulled the blanket tightly around the baby and stared at the gun barrels all around. Last of all came John, carrying little Timothy. Masked men were busy splashing fuel over the mission house and Blazer, getting ready to set them afire.

"Sit on the porch!" the leader ordered gruffly.

Marie looked beyond him into the clear, starry night sky. *Somewhere up there, God is watching us, too,* Marie thought, and her panic was replaced by calm.

The terrorist leader faced the little group of missionaries like a cat ready to torment a mouse between its paws. "You have been teaching the people evil lies!" he declared coldly. "We are going to stop you."

"What lies are we telling the people?" John asked carefully.

"You deceive the people!" insisted the terrorist. "You put false ideas into their heads. You teach them not to help us fight for our rights."

"We don't get involved with politics," John answered quietly. "We only teach God's Word from the Bible."

"I don't believe it!" the gunman snapped. "We know you teach evil lies. You came here to our country to oppress the poor Indians! You are rich Americans, and you steal from the poor."

How unfair! Marie thought, her eyes filling with tears as she remembered the countless hours she had spent caring for the sick in her clinic. What about the many times John and Gary had used their 4-wheel-drive Blazer as an ambulance to take a dying Indian to the faraway city hospital? After all that time they had spent trying to teach the Indians better farming methods; the school and church they had built; and all the quilts and clothing they had given away free, how could this man accuse them so falsely?

"We didn't come to your country to take, we

came to give," John said patiently. "If we wanted to get rich, it would have been better to stay in the United States. We came here because we want to help your people. We spend our time serving them so that they can learn about God!"

"You are rich Americans. You are our enemies," the man in uniform repeated stubbornly. "Your house is ready to burn. Come with us now, down the hill to the church!" he ordered. Fingering his gun threateningly, he shoved the missionaries along the trail to the nearby church building.

The simple cement block and wood structure was quiet and empty in the darkness. Just a few hours before, smiling Indians had crowded in for the Sunday evening service. Pastor John had stood in the lantern-light quoting Philippians 1:21, "For me, to live is Christ, and to die is gain!" Now the church was dark, and the Indian villagers who had heard the gunshots would be hiding, terrified, in their cornfields.

"Set the children down," snapped the guerilla leader, pointing his gun at John and Gary. "Move over there to the fence!"

"No! Please don't hurt them!" cried Marie in anguish.

"Daddy! Daddy!" shrieked the children. "Can't we let them go?" the gunman asked reluctantly, looking at his leader.

"Shoot!" came the stern command.

The terrorist aimed at John and fire flashed from the dark gun barrel as a bullet exploded into the night. Then another and another. Still the wounded man did not fall.

"I can't do it!" the gunman said, turning to his commander.

Angrily, the leader raised his own gun and stepped toward John. As the missionary prayed aloud, the terrorist squeezed the trigger. Seeing the brave missionary fall at last, his killer whirled and fired at Gary. The bullet tore through Gary's chest. "Into Thy hands I commend my spirit," Gary prayed silently as he crumpled to the wet, dewy grass.

Lying motionless, he waited for another bullet, but none came. *If I keep still, they may think I am dead already,* Gary thought with sudden hope. Eyes closed, he listened alertly. Yes, the voices of the attacking guerrillas were fading in the distance as they trooped off up the trail! Soon the silence was broken only by the weeping of Marie and the children as they bent over John's quiet body.

"Daddy is going to be with Jesus," Marie whispered to the little ones. "I want my daddy here!" wailed Timothy. "Those men that shot my daddy are mean. When I get big, I'll shoot them!" declared 5-year-old John Ray.

"No, son," Marie sighed. "Even if we had had ten guns in the house, Daddy would not have shot back at those men. We must love our enemies, because that is Jesus' way. Your Daddy would want us to forgive those men and pray for them." Slowly Gary pulled himself up and looked around. "Gary!" Marie cried softly as he dragged himself painfully over to the others. "Thank God! I thought you were dead too." She covered the shivering man with a blanket.

"I was hit in the chest, but I think the bullet went right through me," Gary said weakly. "Is... is John dead?"

"I'm afraid he's gone," Marie answered softly.

Tears ran down Gary's cheeks. "I'm sorry Marie," he groaned. "If only it had been me instead of John! He had five children to care for."

A chilly wind moaned through the pine trees, and around the sad little group on the mountainside. As Gary stared into the darkness, he wondered where the terrorists had gone. Were they still lurking close by?

"What shall we do now?" Marie asked. "It's too cold out here for the children, and you're hurt. We can't go back up to the house, it's full of spilled kerosene and may explode at any moment."

"I think we ought to go over to Pablo's house," Gary decided. "At least it will be warm there and we will be out of sight."

Slowly the surviving missionaries made their way to the adobe hut where Pablo, a Christian Indian, lived with his family. The door stood open and the house was empty, but Marie's children could snuggle around the fire and fall asleep at last.

Before long Pablo and his family returned from their cornfield where they had fled to hide at the sounds of shooting. They helped Marie give Gary water and coffee to drink, and did their best to make him comfortable.

After praying together, they sat there in silent grief. Nothing more could be done until morning;

it would be too dangerous to venture out on the dark mountain.

Whenever Marie closed her eyes, she seemed to see guns and the body of her husband, lying so still. "Oh, God!" her heart cried. "What will I do now?" But God's love was there, and His strength was ready to uphold her. Gently the Spirit whispered comforting Scriptures to her mind: "We know that all things work together for good to them that love God..." (Romans 8:28). "Fear not therefore, you are of more value than many sparrows." (Luke 12:7).

The night was still dark, but Marie was able to have faith as she waited for the dawn.

Historical Note:
John David Troyer worked in Guatemala for seven years. He was only 28 when he was shot by terrorist gunmen in 1981. Marie and Gary were rescued by fellow missionaries the next day, and Gary was taken to the hospital. Marie and her children returned to the States to live with her parents, but Gary, after he recovered from his gunshot wound, came back to Guatemala for another term of service.

Gary and Marie later married, and Gary became a second father to the Troyer children. The family now lives in North Carolina.

In spite of dangers and hardships, the missions in Guatemala have continued to grow.

This account of John Troyer's murder has been adapted by the author's permission, from the book *Awaiting the Dawn*. To read the rest of this story, order your copy from Christian Light Publications.

18

A MODERN-DAY ELIJAH

"Where can we hold our meetings this evening?" Brother Bob Pierce's face was wrinkled with concern as he faced his Korean friends. Only a small lamp burned in the back room where the ministers were meeting: the two evangelists from America and half a dozen Korean pastors.

Out in the church auditorium, there were no lights at all. Yet more than twelve hundred Korean Christians had already crowded in, to stand praying fervently for the revival meetings which were to begin that night— and it was yet only six o'clock in the morning!

"I don't know," Pastor Chay admitted soberly. "Our church has the largest auditorium in the whole city. But as you saw, it is full this morning with just Christians who have come to pray. We will need to find something else!"

"Can't we meet outdoors?" questioned Brother Findley, the younger evangelist from America.

The Koreans looked at one another and shook their heads. "This is the rainy season," Pastor Park spoke up. "Once rain begins to fall, it will keep raining for days without letting up. There would be no chance of getting the unsaved people to stand outdoors in the pouring rain for a Gospel meeting!"

"There's the railroad station," murmured another of the Korean ministers. "It has a large open courtyard where thousands of people could stand... if only it would not rain!"

Brother Findley bowed his head for a moment. *What is Your will for us, Lord?* he asked silently.

Suddenly the Lord filled his heart with boldness and joy. "I believe God will hold back the rain!" he exclaimed. Looking at Bob Pierce, he saw the same conviction in the other evangelist's eyes.

Brother Bob turned to the Korean pastors. "When you invited us to come for these meetings," he said, "you told us you would trust God to meet all the needs. Let us trust Him now! Go ahead and get permission from the city authorities to use the railroad yard tonight!"

At 11 o'clock the Christians held another meeting in the church. Outside, the rain had already begun. Now as Brother Bob stood behind the pulpit, rain swept against the windows of the church.

"Our meetings will be ruined!" some of the people whispered, looking out at the downpour.

But Brother Bob stood firm in his belief that God was going to work. "I believe with all my heart that God will stop the rain," he told the people, "in time for us to hold the meeting outdoors tonight. Tell everyone you can that God is going to roll back the clouds and give us fair weather this evening!" As he closed the meeting, there was another furious blast of rain.

It was 12:30 noon when Bob Pierce and Brother Findley left the church and dashed through the downpour into the car which took them to their hotel room. Together, they fell on their knees beside the bed and cried out to God for more faith.

"You did it at the Sea of Galilee, Lord," they prayed. "And you did it for Elijah. We know it seems foolish to humans for us to believe that the skies will clear in the middle of the rainy season here in Korea. But we believe that the miracle will happen, bringing glory to the Name of Jesus Christ!"

At 2:30, a wind arose. By 3 o'clock, the skies were almost completely clear. The wind and sun began to dry the muddy surface of the big train courtyard. All over the city of Inchon, Christians fell on their knees again in thanksgiving!

As soon as the last train of the evening had disappeared from the railroad station, crowds of people began to gather. At sundown the rain clouds once more were spreading across the sky, but people still came. Many unbelievers came out of curiosity to see these young American Christians who had dared to promise that God would perform a miracle.

As the evangelists entered the railroad yard that evening, fifteen thousand people stood waiting to hear the message! Throughout the whole service, not a drop of rain fell. Instead, the Koreans eagerly drank in the spiritual rain. Thousands of men, women, and children stood and heard about the power of God to answer prayer and change their hearts. Many Koreans, who were worshipers of the idol called Buddha, became Christians that night.

The next day, threatening rain clouds blanketed the sky once more. Yet by evening they were driven back, and it did not rain! This happened without fail throughout the week.

Finally the farmers around the city of Inchon began to worry. Their main crop was rice, which needs lots of rain to grow in the wet, swampy fields. "The Christians' praying has stopped the rain!" they muttered fearfully. "If the rains don't come this year, our rice crop will die, and we will die of hunger as well! We had better go talk to the pastors and find out when it will rain again."

They came to the Christians, who asked the visiting evangelists for an answer. "What shall we tell our people?" they asked. "When will the rains begin again?"

"Tell the farmers this," replied Brother Findley. "We will pray that our God will keep the storm clouds back only until our meetings close on Sunday night. Then we will pray that God will let the rains come and give them all the water they need."

"We would not dare to ask God to change the weather for any selfish reasons," Brother Pierce added. "But for the sake of the many souls who needed to find Christ at these meetings, we have trusted that God will hold back the rain until the meetings end!"

That night twenty thousand people came to the service. And it did not rain! As the meetings ended, multitudes of people had been given the opportunity to hear God's Word. Hundreds had made their decision to follow Christ.

In the morning, when Brother Bob Pierce rolled out of bed, black clouds were filling the sky. As he journeyed to the airport, the first drops began to fall! He checked in at the ticket office and boarded his plane. Moments later, the pilot taxied his big craft out onto the main runway. As the plane rose into the air, rain came down in such thick sheets that the ground was hardly visible. Brother Bob could well imagine what the farmers of Inchon were talking about!

"Thank you, Lord," he prayed, "for Your showers of blessings. What a great and mighty God You are!"

Historical Note:
Bob Pierce and Bob Findley preached in the Korean city of Inchon in 1950. God, in His wisdom, made it possible for the people of Inchon to hear the message of hope that week, for they were living on the brink of death! Just a few days later, the Communists from North Korea swept into the city in a bloody surprise attack. Inchon is an important seaport city and the Communists knew that if they had Inchon, it would be easy to conquer the rest of Korea.

When the Communists carne, thousands of people were brutally slain.

The city of Inchon soon lay in ruins from the fighting. Churches were destroyed, and Christian pastors were imprisoned and tortured.

For many of the Koreans in the city of Inchon, that week of meetings was their last opportunity to hear the Gospel. And many hundreds of people who met their deaths at the hands of the Communists were able to go to heaven, because they had been saved at those meetings when God held back the rain.

19

A FORTRESS IN THE CHURCH

"We cannot leave the Bible behind," murmured the deacon to his neighbor. "It will be heavy to carry, but it is too precious to leave. I will leave something else behind, but we must have the Bible!"

The two men belonged to a little Armenian church in the mountains of Syria. Terrible persecution had come to the Christians in that land, as the Turks tried to wipe out all who believed in Jesus.

"The Turks are coming this way!" a terrified messenger had cried, and now the whole village was getting ready to leave their valley.

All of the Christian families— men, women and children— must flee over the mountains.

The people were poor. Very few owned a donkey to carry their possessions, so they walked, carrying only the most necessary things. Soon a long line of people straggled along the track to the mountain, pulling their children with them. "Hurry! The Turks are coming! The Turks will kill us!" they repeated over and over.

The church deacon walked with the rest, carrying the treasured Bible. In those days, most Armenian Christians had no Bibles of their own at home, so the church Bible was very precious. And this Bible was an extra-special one, a big, heavy pulpit Bible which had been a gift from the missionary, Elias Riggs.

As the refugees hurried on, the mountain trail grew steep and rocky. "Daddy, carry me!" weary children sobbed. Soon many tired people began leaving their bundles of food and clothing beside the path, for they had no strength left to carry them. The deacon carried the Bible as long as he could. But finally his strength gave out. Tears of weariness rolled down his cheeks as he gently laid the Bible on a rock near the trail.

"Lord, forgive me," he prayed. "Take care of our Bible now, for I cannot!"

Picking up his whimpering child, the deacon staggered on. Night was coming, and the Christians must hurry!

As darkness fell upon the mountainside, a lone mother came up the path with her two children. She had been left behind, for she could not keep up with the others. "I must rest again," the woman groaned. "We can go no farther." Tired legs trembling, she sank down on a rock beside the road.

But something was in the way! Feeling about her in the dark, her hands explored the object's fine leather cover. "This is our church Bible!" she gasped in dismay. "Who could have left it here? Somehow I must take it with me."

After a short rest, the woman wearily rose to her feet. Leaving behind the blanket which she had brought to keep her children warm, she carried the Bible instead. And so, with her baby in one arm and the big Bible in the other, she trudged wearily on.

At last she arrived at the next village. But what was happening? The enemy must be here already! An angry mob of men in red fez hats, waving torches and big knives, milled about in the streets. *The church— I must go to the church,* thought the frightened mother. *Maybe the other Christians will be there.* Slipping among the dark shadows of buildings, she made her way with her children to the back of the village church. Creeping cautiously up to a side door, she knocked softly. "It's me," she said and whispered her name.

Someone unlocked the door and opened it just enough for the woman to slip in with her children. On the floor in the dark church house, several hundred Christians huddled together, their faces terrified.

"Fear not, neighbors— I have our Bible!" whispered the woman, holding up the Book. "She has our Bible!" whispered a man. "She brought the Bible!" glad whispers spread around the room. "Here is a little candle I found," someone murmured softly.

"And I have a match," said another hushed voice.

The Bible was carried into the center of the group, and someone lighted the one little candle with the match. Women close by shaded the small flame with a circle of long skirts, lest its light be seen outside the church. And then into the darkness and fear came a new feeling of God's presence, as one of the Christians began to read in a low voice from Psalm 91:

> "He that dwelleth in the secret place of the Most High, shall abide under the shadow of the Almighty. I will say of the Lord, He is my refuge and my fortress: my God, in Him will I trust. Surely He shall deliver thee... thou shalt not be afraid for the terror by night, nor for the arrow that flieth by day..."

And so they read the promises of God's Word, until the little candle finally burned itself out. Then the people, full of renewed faith in God, lay down and fell asleep where they were on the floor of the church.

For two days and nights the Christians remained in the church. The Turks soon discovered their hiding place, and threatening shouts filled the air. "Come out, Christians, or we'll *burn* you out! You'll never escape from us!"

But the Christians did not reply. "We will stay here," their leaders whispered to one another. "Better to die by fire, together, than to fall into the hands of the cruel Turks. And God is able to save us. He is our refuge and fortress!"

On the third morning, there was silence outside the church. At last there came a timid knock at the door. "The Turks are gone!" called a sympathetic villager. "They left in the night. You are safe, you may come out now!"

It was true. The Turks were gone, and what thanksgiving filled the hearts of the Christians as they came out into the sunshine!

"It was very strange," the villager said to the Christians. "They tried again and again to set the church on fire! Once they even tried to pour kerosene through a hole in the roof to burn you all out. But their fires would never light and every effort failed. I cannot understand it."

But the Christians understood! "God is our refuge and our fortress," they reminded one another happily. "He gave His angels charge over us, and we were safe."

Historical Note:

This miracle happened in 1909, during the massacres of Christians in Armenia by the Turks.

Dr. Elias Riggs, the missionary, died eight years before the story took place. During his sixty-eight years of missionary service, he translated the Bible into the Armenian and Turkish languages. He is said to have had a working knowledge of twenty-one different languages!

20

TEMPLE RUNAWAY

The sun was setting, in clouds of pink and dusty gold. One last burst of light fell upon the huge dark fortress of the Hindu temple as it rose above the narrow street of a village in India.

The temple had been carved from solid rock centuries ago, and the walls and towers were covered with hideous, barbaric figures. There was the Hindu goddess named Kali, her black tongue hanging out, standing on the stone body of a child. Her headdress was made of snakes. In one hand she held a sword, in the other a bloody human head. Next came a statue of the cruel god Shiva, a pitchfork in one hand and the other holding a child he was about to devour. Dozens of other startling and ferociously ugly carvings leered down from their stone settings, but the little girl named Preena did not stop to look at them.

A careless servant had left her door unlocked for once, and the small, slim Indian girl had seen her chance to slip out. Now Preena glanced fearfully up and down the street. It was empty except for a few cows, a bony slinking dog and a beggar who was looking the other way. Preena's heart pounded with a choking excitement. After one last terrified look back into the house beside the temple which she was leaving, the seven-year-old girl broke into a run. Her bare brown feet made no sound on the packed dust of the street.

Preena didn't know where she was going, but she didn't care. Anywhere would be better than the house she was fleeing from, the house across the courtyard from that dark, fearsome stone temple. Ever since Preena was two years old, she had lived in that house with other girls and women who served in the temple. When her father died, Preena's mother had sold her to the temple women to be a slave of the gods. Every day she worked in the temple, carrying lights, firewood and sacrifices, and practicing for hours to perform the devilish dances.

There had been another time when Preena had tried to escape, slipping out into the street when she thought no one was watching. But an evil temple woman had pounced on her almost immediately. "Ungrateful girl!" the woman screeched. "Should a servant of the gods run about in the streets?" and she had dragged Preena back into the courtyard, where she heated an iron rod in the fire and branded her on both hands as a punishment.

After that dreadful day, Preena had served hopelessly for many months. During the day she fetched and carried for the priests as they anointed their idol with oil, decked it with flower garlands, and offered sacrifices before it. All around the idol lay a pool of disgusting muck from rotten sacrifices and human filth. This mud was supposed to be holy, so worshipers must remove their shoes and stand in it barefoot when they prayed to the idol. Often the priests would sacrifice a goat and drink its warm blood before the idol as a crowd of worshipers howled and chanted.

One night as Preena lay on her thin sleeping mat beside the other girls, she overheard two temple women whispering in the darkness.

"...A white woman, one of those Christian missionaries," the priestess whispered. "Her name is Amy, and she steals children from the temples. Once she even dyed her skin brown and sneaked into a temple! She has strong powers from her God, whom they call the Lord Jesus Christ."

"Filthy Christians!" the other temple woman hissed. "She'd better not come into *our* temple. The priests will kill her!"

"Amy, the child stealer... the Lord Jesus Christ." Preena turned these strange words over and over in *her* mind. If only this "Amy" would steal her away from the temple! Was there really any Power which could stand against the power of the temple gods? One tiny sunbeam of hope crept into the dark despair of Preena's life.

But another day Preena overheard words that were much different.

"Preena is seven years old now!" one temple woman cackled to another. "She must be married to the god as soon as possible."

Terror filled the little girl's heart. *What do they mean?* she wondered fearfully. Whatever it was, it must be bad. Preena had heard the screams of other children in that temple on hot dark nights, when the drums pounded and clouds of incense filled the air like an evil drug. Would she be left alone in there some night, tied to the idol in the dark? What might that ugly black idol do to her? More desperately than ever, Preena had watched for a chance to escape.

Now she dashed down a side street and out to the edge of the village. Like any child who has lived all her life locked behind high walls, Preena knew little about the world outside. A stream flowed past, and she looked at it in surprise. So much water! Stepping carefully down the bank, she waded across to the other side; then trotted through a grove of palm trees and on down the road. Soon darkness would be falling, when tigers and other wild animals would come out to seek their prey. Could Preena make it to another village? If she did, would anyone help her there?

Dusk was falling as the little girl reached the next village. An old woman carrying a jar of water from the well noticed her and stopped. "Child, where are you going?" she asked.

"I'm looking for the child-catching Amy," Preena replied timidly. "Do you know where she lives?"

Several other people rose from their places around their supper fires and came to stare at the strange girl. "Look at her clothes!" cried a woman. "She is a temple girl. A slave of the gods, running away!" "Grab her!" a man shouted.

Threatening faces were all around, and many hands reached out to grab the runaway! Gasping, Preena whirled around and fled in panic. Fear gave wings to her feet as she turned down another street.

Suddenly a woman stepped out of a doorway in front of Preena. A light-skinned woman! Could this be the "Amy" she was looking for?

"Help me!" Preena shrieked, hurling herself into the strange white woman's arms. "I don't want to be a slave of the gods! I want the Lord Jesus Christ!"

The white woman's arms tightened around Preena, as she faced the child's pursuers. "What does this mean?" she asked sternly.

"She belongs to the temple! She has run away! Give her to us!" cried the mob. Trembling, Preena clung to the missionary. Her heart sank as she caught a glimpse of three temple women pushing their way through the crowd. Jewelry glittered around their necks and arms. Their eyes, too, glittered cruelly in their painted faces.

"She is ours," the oldest announced coldly. "We paid fifty rupees for that girl and she is ours. Give her to us!"

But the missionary would not yield. Her eyes flashed like swords as she stood firm with her arms around Preena.

"The child has claimed my help in the Name of my Lord Jesus Christ," she said firmly. "I will repay you your fifty rupees, but this girl you may not have."

A policeman arrived and watched as the missionary handed money to the temple women. "Everyone go home," he ordered, waving his arms and the crowd scattered away.

Preena could hardly believe what had happened. She still clung to the missionary with both hands as she was led gently into a house. Sitting down, the white-skinned woman took Preena onto her lap.

"My name is Amy," she told the tired little girl. "You don't need to be afraid any more. I have bought your freedom! And tomorrow I will tell you all about the Lord Jesus Christ, Who also wants to set you free."

Historical Note:

Amy, in this story, was Amy Carmichael, an Irish missionary, who spent 53 years in India. She saved nearly a thousand children like Preena from slavery and moral danger in the Hindu idol temples. Amy founded a Christian village, called Dohnavur Fellowship, where these children could be taught and cared for in safety.

When Amy was a little girl, she prayed that God would turn her brown eyes into blue eyes like her mother's. God did not give Amy her request, and when she grew up, she found out the reason! A blue-eyed woman could never have gained entrance to many of the places in India where Amy was able to go. God created Amy with brown eyes, knowing that someday she would need to look as much like an Indian woman as possible.

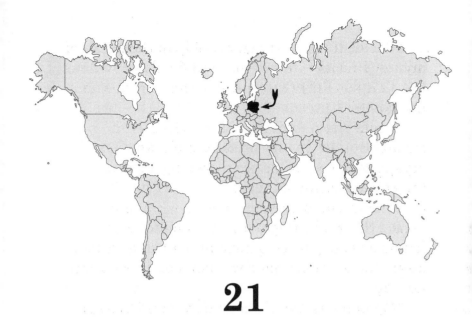

21

ONLY ONE PAGE

Wearily, Robert Evans closed his tired, red-rimmed eyes. His hands shook as he folded them over his Bible where it lay on the pulpit. He had been preaching for six and a half hours!

"I cannot preach any more now," he whispered hoarsely to the Polish interpreter. "Sorry, but I must have a rest."

Robert was a minister from America, bringing the Gospel to the suffering people of Poland in the days just after World War II. Tonight he had preached in the town hall of a city in Eastern Poland. The hall was packed with people; people standing in the aisles, sitting in the windows, and even crowding the platform so tightly that Robert had not been able to move his feet while he preached. But thousands more waited outside!

Time after time, ushers had emptied the building and let in a new crowd of people hungry to hear the Gospel. Robert and his Russian and Polish interpreters preached to each group in turn, as the hours slipped by.

As Brother Evans preached of Jesus' saving power, hundreds of people responded gladly to the message. So many of them had never heard these Bible truths before!

It was long past midnight when Robert Evans finally ended the meeting. Outside in the darkness waited another great crowd who had not been able to get in. Robert's heart was heavy as he made his way through these hundreds of people who had not yet heard the message of the Savior!

An old man reached out from the crowd and tugged at Robert's sleeve. Talking excitedly in Russian, he hung on so persistently that the preacher stopped.

"What is he saying?" Robert asked his Russian interpreter.

"He has a piece of paper," the interpreter replied, "and he wants you to tell him whether it is from the Bible."

The old man was wrinkled, shriveled, and bent from many years of toil. Slowly and carefully his gnarled fingers pulled out a small cloth bundle from his inner coat pocket. Unwrapping the cloth, he reverently held up a folded paper. The paper's edges were ragged from much handling and yellow with age.

"Why, it's a page from the Book of Exodus!" the interpreter exclaimed.

"I have read this page over and over again for many years," said the old man, with a quaver in his voice. "I thought it must be from the Bible, but I was never sure. I only knew it was something holy. But I have always wondered, what does the rest of the Book say? What comes on the next page?" Tears spilled over and ran down the wrinkled cheeks.

Wordlessly, Robert held out his own Bible to the old man, who took it as gently as he would have held a baby. Turning it over in his hands, he carefully thumbed through a few pages. Peering at the words, he shook his head and murmured, "I cannot read this! It is not my language. But, oh, this is the first time in all my eighty years that I have seen a Bible!"

As Robert Evans trudged back to his lodging place for the night, he thought of all the Bibles in his own country. There were Bibles in the churches, Bibles in the bookstores, and Bibles in homes where people didn't even bother to read them. *It isn't fair!* he thought. *I have many Bibles, in different sizes and translations, in my home... while he has only one page.*

Historical Note:

Robert Evans was born to missionary parents in Cameroun, West Africa. When he grew up, Robert became concerned about the multitudes of people in Europe who had never heard the Gospel. In 1952, he started the European Bible Institute, which has continued to send missionaries and Bibles to the spiritually hungry people of Europe.

22

DAY OF DISASTER

On March 27, 1964, a mighty earthquake struck Alaska. Sliding rock layers underground made the land shake like a dog shakes a rat! Mountains quivered and split apart. Highways and sidewalks rippled in waves of concrete. Buildings in the city of Anchorage dropped as much as thirty feet down when the ground beneath them simply fell away.

"When the dust cleared," remembers a lady from Kansas who was visiting Alaska that day, "we looked out at the apartment house next door and couldn't believe our eyes! Between that building and ours, there was an enormous crack in the earth, 20 feet wide! A man was standing in his open door, looking straight down into the hole where his porch had been."

But more disaster was coming! Out in the ocean depths, where the earthquakes had disturbed the waters, giant waves formed and rushed toward the land. Soon a wall of water thirty feet high came thundering up the channel into the Gulf of Alaska, to hit the islands and tiny fishing villages.

Fisherman John Larsen was out in his little boat not far from the island of Afognak, when he saw the wave approaching. "I see something coming... something big!... this is a *big one!*" he shouted urgently into his radio. Then his transmitter was silenced forever, as the huge wave overtook his boat.

Most of the Indians on Afognak Island received his warning just in time to save their lives by escaping to higher ground. But out of thirty-eight homes on the island, twenty-three were shattered and washed away by the wave.

Ten days later Noah Miller[1], a carpenter from Canada, sat in church listening as his minister made an announcement.

"The Mennonite Disaster Service is asking for volunteers," said the minister, "to help rebuild a small Indian village in the flooded area of Alaska. Over four thousand people have lost their homes because of the earthquake and flood in Alaska!"

Noah shivered slightly, thinking of all those people who had escaped with their lives only to see their homes lie in ruins. Where would all those poor men, women, and children sleep at night? Alaska was a cold place!

I believe I'll go, Noah thought. *And maybe I'll*

1. not his real name

have an opportunity to tell some of those Indians about Jesus, too.

The Mennonite Disaster Service leaders had flown to Alaska after the quake, to see where their men could help. They learned that people in big cities like Anchorage were getting plenty of aid from the government and other organizations. But who would help the homeless Indians, in poor villages like Afognak?

"We will bring carpenters, plumbers, and electricians, and help rebuild this village," the men decided. Soon Noah Miller and thirty-nine other volunteers from churches in the United States and Canada were on their way to Alaska. They brought their tools, and they came to build!

First the land had to be cleared of fallen trees and broken parts of houses and boats. The flood waters had lifted heavy fishing boats and crab boats like empty peanut shells, flinging them over the harbor and up onto land.

Next the men dug holes for pilings, set the floor joists, and the houses began to grow! Sawdust flew through the air as saws whined and hammers banged briskly. The Mennonite volunteers often sang or whistled as they worked, and soon the shy Indian children crowded around to watch these friendly strangers.

"My name is Noah," Noah Miller told an Indian boy when he came down from the roof for more nails. "What's your name?"

"Noah?" the boy repeated, and a gleam of mischief came into his eyes. "Are you the same Noah who built the ark in that other flood? A preacher came here once and told us about him."

"No, I'm not that same Noah," the carpenter chuckled. "I'm just a relative of his. But God who kept Noah safe in his ark is the same God who has kept you safe through this flood in Afognak!"

Besides working on new homes for the Indians, the Christian carpenters built a small church house with a pulpit and a table for Communion. In the evenings after work, they gathered together for services there. "We have come to help you in the name of Christ," they told the people of Afognak. "We would like to tell you more about Him, too!"

Before Noah knew it, his six weeks of work on Afognak Island were over. Seven of the new houses were completely done, and the others could be finished by the Indians themselves.

Noah had another project, too, that was not quite finished. He had made friends with one of the men of Afognak, and spoken to him about his soul. The Indian had shown interest in Noah's Gospel message, but still had not made his decision for Christ!

"How can I witness to him one more time, Lord?" Noah prayed. "Please give me a chance to speak with him alone, before we leave."

It was not long before Noah's prayer was answered. "Mister Noah, I would like to take you for a ride in my boat tomorrow before you leave," his Indian friend invited. "We can go see one of the little islands, and catch a few fish. Would you like to do that?"

"Sure!" Noah accepted happily. *This must be*

the Lord's answer to my prayer, he thought.

The next morning was clear and sunny. The small motorboat churned up a wake of white water through the blue waves. "What a beautiful day!" Noah exclaimed.

Seven miles from Afognak, a small island loomed ahead. "There's the place we're heading for," the Indian told Noah. "Soon we will—" he stopped abruptly. The motor on the boat was sputtering! It gave one final cough and died. Calmly the Indian checked different parts of the motor, then turned to Noah. "I can't fix it," he apologized. "We'd better start rowing to the island; look, a fog is coming in."

It was true. Noah's heart sank as he looked up at the disappearing sky and then at the small faraway island. Could they row that far before the fog covered them completely? And how would they ever be rescued from the island? Frantically, the men worked their oars. Their only hope was to reach the island while they could still see it! Grimly, the thick fog rolled closer and closer across the water.

At last the men made their way through shallow waves and drew the boat up onto the little beach. "Now what do we do?" Noah asked.

"Now we wait," the Indian replied. "Someone will come by with a boat, or the fog will lift if we wait long enough." Several hours passed, and still there was no sign of rescue. The men grew hungry, so the Indian scouted along the ground until he found a nest of ptarmigan eggs. Kindling a small fire, he roasted the eggs in its ashes.

"You know," he said to Noah as they ate their strange meal, "You aren't like a lot of white men. Most white men would get all upset about being stranded like this, and having their plans turned upside down!"

Here was the chance Noah had been waiting for.

"Being a Christian gives a man peace," he told his friend earnestly. "We don't need to be fearful or upset, because we know God is in control of everything. Even if we die, we will be safe in heaven. God will give you this faith too if you ask him. Would you like to do that?"

"Yes, I would," the Indian said huskily. "Will you pray with me?"

What a thrill of joy filled Noah's heart as the two men knelt on that rocky shore in Alaska!

Just as they rose from their knees, the roar of a motorboat sounded faintly in the distance. "I must make a signal fire, so they will know where to find us," the new Christian Indian stated. Taking his can of gasoline, he poured some onto the beach and set a match to it. With a *whoosh*, orange flames leaped high in the air! Out in the fog, the sound of a motor changed direction as the boat turned toward their fire.

God was in control of everything, Noah thought gladly. *He allowed the boat to break down for a reason, and now He sends rescue at just the right moment. God can bring souls to salvation, even through disaster!*

Historical Note:

The Mennonite Disaster Service is an organization that provides Christian volunteers to work wherever they are needed. When any natural disaster such as flood, hurricane, earthquake, or tornado strikes in the United States or overseas, MDS is ready to go.

The motto of MDS is the Scripture verse: "Bear ye one another's burdens, and so fulfill the law of Christ." Each volunteer worker wears a blue and white badge showing two clasped hands beneath a cross.

No one but God knows how many thousands of men and women have volunteered, like "Noah Miller" in the story, to work with Mennonite Disaster Service.

Before the volunteers left Afognak Island, the chief of the Indian village there made an announcement. "This stream, which flows past our new village, shall be called 'Mennonite Creek'!" he said. And "Mennonite Creek" it still is named today.

23

THE BOY WHO WAS DETER-

MINED

"I wonder what kind of nest that could be? Surely I can get it for my collection!"

Young William Carey, a short, stocky boy of nine or ten years old, stood beneath a tall chestnut tree, peering up into the branches.

Autumn was settling richly over the South of England. The leaves and prickly burred nuts of the tree were turning dry and brown and William knew that the nest would be empty. Setting one boot firmly against the tree trunk, he grabbed a low-hanging branch and started up.

William loved to study nature. Whenever he was not busy at school or doing chores for his parents, the young boy would wander through the woods and fields. He studied birds, animals, and plants. If there was any new kind of bird or plant that William did not know, he was eager to discover it!

The nest he wanted now was quite high up in the tree, but William was determined to have it. Digging his toes into the knots and crevasses of the rough gray bark, he hauled himself from one branch to another. Suddenly, a chunk of bark gave way beneath his foot! With a smothered cry of alarm, William lost his grip and slid down the trunk. Thud! His boots struck the ground.

"Owww!" William breathed softly, looking at his hands. They had been scraped almost raw by the rough bark as he slid down. He blew gently on each sore palm and turned to look upward. The nest still sat securely on the branch.

It might be a sparrow's nest, but which kind? William wondered. *I have to see it closer!* and again he started to climb the tree.

But poor William. Once more he fell, before he had climbed very far! The nest seemed to be mocking his efforts. Should he give up?

"No, I'm *going* to have that nest!" William decided. Grasping the rough bark again, he began to climb the tree for the third time.

Now, at last, it seemed as though victory was in sight. William had made his way up to the branch where the nest was perched, and began to crawl carefully out along the limb. The nest sat in a fork where the branch divided and sloped downward, and William felt sure he could reach it. Only a stubby stick of dead wood blocked his way! Lying full length along his limb, William took hold of the rotten stick to break it off.

Snap! As the stick gave way in his hand, William lost his balance. "No!" he cried, clutching desperately for a hold among the branches. But it was no use. With terrible force, he crashed to the ground!

"Ohhh, my leg!" William moaned. Flashes of pain shot through it, making him feel sick to his stomach. After resting for awhile, he tried to walk, but found it impossible. Sinking back to the grass, he began calling for help.

"Papa! PAPA!" he called first, but there was no reply. His father, the village schoolmaster, must be indoors preparing lessons. So William called for his mother, and then his sister Mary. Finally his cries were heard and the injured boy was carried home to the school house where his family lived. The doctor was sent for, and William's mother clucked sadly over her son as he lay in his bed.

Weeks passed, and William's broken leg began to heal. As he sat indoors reading or hobbled about the yard, he often thought of that nest up in the chestnut tree.

I must get that nest! the boy thought stubbornly. *When I start something like that, I cannot bear to give it up!* At last the day came when he could walk well enough to slip out of his yard and through the field. His steps led him straight to the foot of that chestnut tree. By now the branches were mostly bare of leaves, but sure enough, the troublesome nest was still there!

Without a backward glance, William seized a branch and began climbing. His injured leg was still weak, and wrapped in a clumsy bandage, so he climbed slower this time. Cautiously William inched his way out along the limb. Closer and closer he crawled, until at last his fingers closed tightly around the prize for which he had risked so much! A slow smile of satisfaction spread over William's face as he tucked the precious nest inside his jacket front.

William's parents were anxiously watching for him as he limped wearily into the house. "Where have you been, son?" his father asked.

"I was getting that nest," said the boy triumphantly, holding up the little swirl of straw and twigs.

"You mean you climbed *that* tree again?" cried his mother.

"I couldn't help it, Mother," he replied. "When I begin something, I must go through with it!"

"Whatever William starts, he finishes," said sister Mary, admiringly.

And that was the secret of William Carey's life. When he grew up, he became a school teacher like his father, and a minister of the Gospel. He became very concerned about the souls of the heathen in faraway lands who had no chance to hear about Christ. Sometimes, as he taught Geography lessons in his school, he would burst into tears.

"Children, the people in those countries are heathens!" he would cry, pointing to the map. "They are lost, millions of them, without the blessed Savior!"

At a ministers' meeting, William asked his fellow preachers, "Don't you think Jesus' command to 'Go ye therefore and teach all nations' is still for us today?"

There was a strange silence. Christians in those days in England did not like to think about foreign missions!

At last the leading elder said sternly, "Young man, sit down. When God pleases to convert the heathen, He won't need any help from us!"

But the boy who was determined had grown up to be a determined man, too. Finally he gathered a group of twelve ministers who agreed with him that the Gospel should be carried throughout the world. The Missionary Society they started in 1792 was an important beginning for modern missions.

Then William Carey learned of a Christian doctor who wanted to start a mission in India. *What an opportunity!* he thought. *Now who shall we send to India, to help in the work?*

Turning to the fifty-fourth chapter of Isaiah, William saw six words which seemed to stand out in letters of fire. "For the Lord hath called thee." "FOR THE LORD HATH CALLED THEE!"

It was the Lord speaking to him, William knew. "*You* are the one to go!" And William Carey obeyed. Together with his wife and four children, his wife's sister, and Dr. John Thomas, he set sail for India in the summer of 1793.

Now, William needed every bit of the determination and strength he had! For the people of India were not eager to turn from their darkness and cruel customs to the Light of the Gospel. They feared to become Christians, lest their families cast them out. William and Dr. Thomas worked patiently and lovingly, year after year. They preached and taught and witnessed, brought healing to the sick and translated Scriptures into many of the languages of India.

Many men would have given up after a few years and returned home to comfortable England. But William Carey, the determined boy, was also a man of determination. As the years rolled by, he remained steadfast where the Lord had called him.

At last, after 7 years, he found a man named Krishna Pal, a Hindu carpenter, who was willing to suffer for Jesus and be baptized in His name. Only one man, but he was the first of a mighty harvest! God had a great work, and great rewards, for the boy who was determined.

Historical Note:
William Carey's favorite motto was "Expect Great Things from God! Attempt Great Things for God!" He was the leader of Christian missions in India for 41 years. With the help of his wife Charlotte and other associates, he translated the Word of God; either the whole Bible or portions of the Bible, into thirty-four different languages.

24

A DUST PAN FOR JESUS

"Preacher, may I go with you to the mission?" the young African boy begged. "I want to learn about Jesus, and how to read the Bible like you do."

Raymond Bush, the missionary, looked in surprise at the earnest face of the boy. "What is your name, my boy?" he asked. "And do you have permission from your parents and your chief to go along with me?"

"I am called Tisese," the boy replied. "Will you take me, if I am allowed to go?"

The missionary promised that he would, and so the next morning a very happy Tisese followed along with Raymond Bush and his men. It was a long way from Tisese's village in the interior of Africa back to the mission station. For nine weeks, the group of men and boys traveled through jungles, plains, and desert sand. The days were long and tiring, but very exciting to a young boy who had never been far from his home village before. The wooded lands were full of monkeys, giraffe, and elephants. On the plains, lions stalked herds of zebra and antelopes, while ostriches ran awkwardly through the tall grass. Clumps of thorn bushes were everywhere. The Africans called these "Wait-a-bit thorns" because when you were caught in them, your friends had to wait a bit!

Night time was scary for a young boy. Their camp had to be surrounded by a ring of fire all through the night for protection from wild animals and mosquitoes. The men would cut timber, pile it all around the camp and set fire to it. During the night, the fire was kept burning, and although lions roared in the darkness outside, the travelers within the circle were safe.

At last they arrived at the mission station, where Raymond Bush lived. Now Tisese could finally go to school! How he loved to learn. Eagerly his quick mind drank in the stories of Jesus and all the truths of God's Word. When he was not in school learning, he would follow the missionaries around at their work, asking questions. "Tisese, you ask more questions in an hour than I can answer in a week!" Raymond said one day.

But Tisese was not embarrassed. There were so many new things to see and learn, he just *had* to ask questions! "What is that thing you are sweeping the dirt into?" he asked Mrs. Bush one morning as she swept the floor of her hut. "This is called a dustpan," the missionary's wife replied.

"Thank you!" called the boy as he hurried past on his way to school. Slipping into his seat, he waited for class to begin. As soon as the teacher called his name, Tisese rose to his feet. "Teacher," he told the missionary solemnly, "I want you and everyone to know that my name is no longer Tisese, 'the-animal-which-runs-through-the-woods'. Now that I am a Christian, my name shall be 'Dust Pan' forever!"

"Dust Pan?" the teacher exclaimed, surprised. "Why ever would you want your name to be *Dust Pan?*"

"Because, Teacher," the boy replied earnestly, "I was just passing your house and saw your wife sweeping, with that tool called a dust pan in her hand. She carried all the dirt out of your hut with it. I want to be a dust pan, too, so that when I go home I may carry out the dirt from the lives of my father, my family, and all my friends. I want to be a Dust Pan for Jesus!"

From that day on, the boy could often be heard praying that God would make him a good dust-pan for His service. Soon he had brought five of his friends to Jesus, and the six Christian boys together witnessed to others.

Time passed and one day Raymond Bush was preparing to take another evangelistic journey into the north country where Dust Pan's village lay.

"Now, I can go home and tell my family the Good News about Jesus!" Dust Pan said joyfully.

"No, Dust Pan," the missionary objected.

"You are still young. You should stay here in

school for a few years yet, and my wife will need you to help her while I am gone."

"Preacher, I *must* go now!" cried Dust Pan. "There is no time to lose! Even now my family could be dying without Jesus. My father could be killed in a tribal fight. My mother may be eaten by lions while working in the garden! My brothers and sisters may die and never hear of Jesus in time."

"All right, my boy," the missionary relented. "You shall go along, and may God bless you as you try to be a Dust Pan to your people!"

Once more Dust Pan traveled the weary and dangerous miles through the African jungles following elephant and hippopotamus trails. Through burning desert sands the caravan plodded, until Dust Pan's feet were sore and covered with blisters. One night the boy lay moaning with pain as the missionary tried to treat his blistered feet.

"You cannot walk any farther with such sore feet, my boy," Mr. Bush said sadly. "I will leave you here with the chief of this village and pay him to care for you until your feet heal. You can go along with me to your village next year."

"No, no! I must go with you now!" Dust Pan insisted. "My father may be killed in tribe fighting. My mother might be eaten by lions while she works in the garden. My brothers and sisters might die before next year, and never hear of Jesus!"

So when the travelers went on the next morning, the determined Dust Pan came limping along with them!

The trail that morning led through miles of tall grass, called elephant grass. Suddenly as the path took them around a sharp bend, a lioness sprang from a clump of grass stems! In one awful instant, she pounced upon a servant who was carrying a box of supplies for the missionary. With a cry, the man dodged and the lion's paws struck the box on his back, sending it rolling into the tall grass. Jerking up the shotgun that he carried, Mr. Bush fired! In the excitement, he missed. Hissing horribly, the lioness disappeared into the tall grass.

Feeling shaky, but thankful, after their narrow escape, the mission party continued on. Their water supply was low, so they were in a hurry to get to the river. At last, late in the afternoon, they reached their goal. As his men pitched their tents and refilled the water bottles, the missionary counted them. One was missing!

"Where is Dust Pan?" he called in alarm. "Dust Pan is not with us! When did you see him last?" But nobody knew.

"Maybe the lioness got him," one man ventured. "If he's out there in the grass alone, he's been eaten by now," others muttered. "There's no use going back to find him!"

"What shall we do, Lord?" cried Raymond, falling to his knees in prayer. *I've already had two men killed by lions during my travels,* he thought. *I don't want to lose Dust Pan!* "Lord, I know that You can do anything," he prayed. "Please protect this boy somehow, and save him for the work he wanted to do!"

As the missionary paced around and around

the camp, he strained his eyes searching for any sign of movement among the tall grasses. Far away a lion roared its horrible, coughing roar, and a shiver went down the spines of all the listeners!

The sun was sinking behind the hills, when the anxious missionary finally saw the grasses waving along the paths where they had travelled. Running forward eagerly, he cried, "Dust Pan! Are you safe, my boy?"

Staggering wearily out of the elephant grass, Dust Pan lifted his hands in triumph. "God kept me alive, to tell my parents about Jesus!"

When the relieved missionary reached his young friend, though, he saw a sad sight. Even though Dust Pan's sore feet had been bandaged and padded with dry grass, the blisters had burst as he walked and his feet were now bleeding with every step he took. It was no wonder he had not been able to keep up to the others!

Raymond Bush called for his men and together they carried the tired boy the rest of the way into camp. Kneeling before him, the missionary did what he could for poor Dust Pan's bloody feet. "Lord," he prayed humbly, "what a love for souls is in this boy's heart! He is a better missionary than I am. Help me to be more like Dust Pan!"

When Dust Pan finally reached his home village, the battle had only begun. His father was one of the most famous witch doctors in that part of Africa, and usually killed more than six hundred people every year! In his heathen cruelty, he put to death anyone who offended him by poisoning them, burying them alive, or tying them to ant hills and letting the ants eat them. Was there any use in hoping that such an evil man would become a Christian?

But Dust Pan's faith and love won the hearts of his whole family— even that father! Both his parents, his three sisters, and all five brothers were converted and became Christians. Then Dust Pan began to share the Gospel with others in his village. When Raymond Bush returned the following year, he found three hundred and sixty-four new Christians waiting to be baptized, all through the witness of one young boy.

What a lot of sin, darkness, and dirt had been carried out of that corner of Africa, by one Dust Pan in the hands of Jesus!

Historical Note:

Raymond L. Bush was an American missionary to South Africa in the early 1900's. The story of the boy named Dust Pan is recorded in his autobiography, *Thinking Africa.*

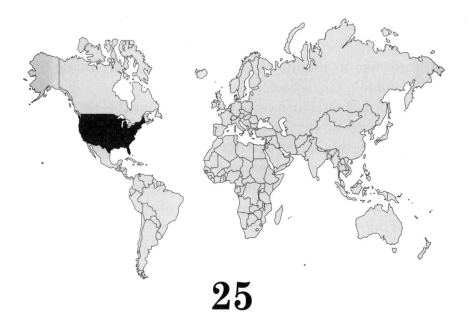

25

The Man with the Gospel Papers

"Friend, will you have a Gospel paper?" Ralph Palmer held out a small tract to the man passing on the sidewalk in front of him.

Surprised, the stranger looked up. He saw a big man wearing a friendly smile. The paper booklet in his hand was printed neatly with the title: *Four Things God Wants You To Know.*

"Yes, sir, thank you," the stranger replied. *I do need to find out more about God,* he thought, as he walked on down the street. *My doctor just told me this morning that I don't have long to live. God must have sent that man to give me this paper!* A tear slipped from one eye and trickled down his cheek.

Meanwhile, Ralph still stood in his place on the sidewalk, busily passing out Gospel tracts to all who came by. It was a fine spring day in New-port News, Virginia, one of the world's greatest harbor cities. Ships come and go in its port, carry-ing cargoes to and from all parts of the world. *I wonder how many of my tracts are carried by sail-ors to faraway countries?* Ralph mused.

He slipped several more tracts from the bun-dle in his left arm and held them ready in his right hand. Another crowd of people was approaching along the street and Ralph wanted to be prepared!

"Friend, will you have a Gospel paper?"

"No, I won't! Get out of my way!" snapped a surly-looking young man. "Why don't you stay off the streets with that junk?"

Ralph only nodded courteously and turned to meet the next person.

A well-dressed woman came near, and Ralph offered her a tract. Sudden anger flared in her face, and she stamped her foot. "Don't you *ever* ask me to take one of those things again!" she cried. "I've already had two of them and I tell you I don't want any more."

Another man accepted a paper, only to tear it to bits and throw them into Ralph's face! Laugh-ing evilly, he hurried away.

Ralph sighed and breathed a prayer for for-giveness for those foolish people who would not think of their souls. How suddenly they could be brought before God's Judgment! How well Ralph remembered the engineer on the C & O Railroad. Back in the days when Ralph worked for the railroad, it had been his job to inspect the air brakes on locomotives and passenger cars. Late one night, after he had finished inspecting an extra-long train, Ralph climbed up into the locomotive and spoke to the engineer. After exchanging a few friendly words, Ralph handed him a couple of tracts.

"You give me some of these little papers every time you see me, don't you?" the engineer laughed as he stuffed the tracts into his shirt pocket. The whistle blew and Ralph swung out of the cab.

That train was headed for Richmond and made good time. The engineer was a man of many years' experience and handled it skillfully. He slowed down at the proper time as they neared curves in the track and opened the throttle on long, straight stretches. All at once, though, his fireman began to notice that the train was not slowing down when it should. Some dangerous curves were coming up ahead, but the engineer did not slacken his speed.

"Aren't you going too fast, Sir?" the fireman shouted.

There was no answer. The engineer was sitting straight up with his head bent forward, apparently watching the track. Had he fallen asleep at the throttle?

"Wake up!" the fireman shouted again. "You are going too fast!"

Still there was no reply. The fireman grabbed the engineer's shoulder and shook him— then jumped back, horrified. The engineer was dead! His lifeless body slumped over and fell to the floor. The fireman threw a brake lever and stopped the train. Other crew members climbed into the cab and helped him drive slowly into the next station.

A doctor was called, but it was too late. The engineer's heart had stopped beating and he had gone suddenly to face the judgment, with Ralph's tracts still unread in his shirt pocket.

Now Ralph bowed his head as he stood on the sidewalk. *Help me, Lord, to reach more people with Your message before it's too late!* he prayed. Another handful of tracts ready, he stepped forward as more people came out of a nearby store. "Friend, won't you have a Gospel paper?" he asked politely.

Two little black girls, with freshly braided hair, came walking along hand-in-hand. The older one took a tract, then said: "Mister, can we give you some money to help you buy the tracts you pass out? Mother said we may give you something."

"Why, that would be very nice, if you want to help pay for the tracts!" Ralph smiled at the children.

After feeling around in her purse, the little girl held out two nickels.

"Thank you, girls, and God bless you," Ralph told them as they skipped happily away.

Here comes a police officer, Ralph said to himself a few minutes later. *I wonder what he wants?*

The officer approached Ralph and held out his hand with a friendly smile. "I suppose you are Mr. Palmer," he said.

At Ralph's reply, he went on, "One of my secretaries brought me a tract with your name and address on the back. I came by to tell you we are glad for your work in our town. The whole police force appreciates what you are doing, Mr. Palmer!"

Ralph chuckled to himself after the policeman

had gone on down the street. He was remembering another town, where the police had actually arrested him for passing out Gospel tracts. *There are a lot of adventures in my work for the Lord,* Ralph thought.

He remembered a day when he had stood in the freezing wind on the corner of Granby Street in Norfolk. It was the 23rd of December. Shoppers were crowding the streets and sidewalks, hurrying to get all their Christmas buying done. Ralph's hands moved constantly in the cold air as he held out little tracts to people rushing by.

From morning until supper time, Ralph worked, passing out about nine thousand Gospel papers. But as the day wore on, he began to get discouraged. So many people took the papers only to drop them underfoot on the street as soon as they walked away! The sidewalks around him were littered with hundreds of wasted tracts. The men and women of Norfolk were not interested in God's message of salvation. Why not just give up?

It was late when Ralph reached home, tired, cold and hungry. "I'm *never* going to Norfolk again!" he announced to his wife. "Those people aren't interested, so I may as well not waste anymore time and money on tracts for them. They throw away more tracts than any other city I've seen!"

But first thing the next morning, Ralph told his wife that he was going back to Norfolk.

"Norfolk!" she exclaimed. "I thought you said..."

"I know," Ralph interrupted. "But I was wrong. The Lord told me that I should go back there today!" So on the last day before Christmas, Ralph once more handed out thousands of tracts on Granby Street.

About two months later, the Palmers received a letter from Florida. Here is what it said:

Dear Brother Palmer,

> For thirteen years my husband was an alcoholic. Many times, I had to take our three children and flee from his threats. I had prayed for him, so long!
>
> Last Christmas he left us and went to Norfolk, Virginia, to visit his buddy, who also drinks. As they walked down Granby Street toward a liquor store, on the night before Christmas, a man handed them two Gospel tracts. They put them into their pockets and when my husband got to his friend's house, he began to read. For the first time in his life, he saw what was wrong with him and who his enemy was. He pushed back the whiskey bottle and said,
>
> "You can have this, Ted. I'm finished with it!" He went right away and caught a train to come home.
>
> Now my husband is a Christian, and I thank you from the depths of my soul, Brother Palmer! You saved our family, all because you passed out tracts that day. We praise God for this mighty work!
>
> —Mrs. H.

Ralph smiled as he remembered that happy

letter. *Even if only one man was saved, out of nine thousand people who took my tracts that day, it would be worth it,* he thought.

"Would you like a Gospel paper?" he asked a man who was coming near.

"No, sir!" The man scowled and waved Ralph away.

"Friend, will you have a Gospel paper?" Ralph asked the next person approaching.

"Yes, sir! Thank you, thank you!" this one replied.

It's just like Jesus' parable of the Sower who sowed His seed: some falls on good soil, and some upon stony ground, Ralph mused. "Lord, I pray that Your work may bring forth fruit!"

Historical Note:
Ralph Palmer faithfully sowed the seed. During his lifetime he personally handed out over 10 million tracts, which would make a pile weighing more than 20 tons. Sometimes he passed out ten thousand in a day, which would average one tract every three seconds.

His Gospel tracts were carried all over the world by people who received them, and he had letters from people as far away as Japan.

Ralph and his wife Martha also made thousands of Gospel signs with letters that glowed in the dark to place along busy highways. Many thousands of people who drove past these signs, read the messages over and over again: "You Must Be Born Again!" "Where Will You Spend Eternity?" or "Christ Died For Your Sins!"

Ralph Palmer lived in Virginia until his death in 1976.

If you would like to know more of his life story, read *A Sower Went Forth*, Rod & Staff Publishers.

26

THE MISSIONARY SAYS A

BAD WORD

Pedro was just six years old, and he was terribly frightened. Under the thin, ragged shirt he wore, his heartbeat fluttered against his ribs. Brown eyes wide, he stared at the big boy who was speaking.

"It's true!" the older boy repeated with a mocking grin. "Pepe heard the principal talking. You little boys are going to be sent to the foreign missionaries' Home, because you're too small to live here at the Observatory. Those foreigners are Gringos, white people from the United States. And you know why they have pale white skin instead of a brown skin like ours?" The big boy leaned closer, and hissed, "It's because they eat children! They will fatten you up until you're nice and plump and then—" the boy drew a finger across his throat and rolled his eyes horribly— "they will eat you!"

Pedro was too scared to reply. He stared mutely, eyes bright with unshed tears, as the big boy walked away laughing to join his friends. *I wonder if Alfredo is going to that place, too?* he thought. *He is little like me!*

Pedro had never known much love in his short life. He had no idea where his parents were, or whether he even had any parents. He could just barely remember being brought to town several years before, by a man who had disappeared, leaving him all alone on the city street. Could that man have been Pedro's father? If so, why had he left him behind? Pedro didn't know. He had cried himself to sleep on the sidewalks and stolen food to eat when he was hungry, until at last a policeman had picked him up and brought him to the Boys' Observatory. About 300 boys lived in the Observatory, penned up behind a large chainlink fence. Most of them were much older than Pedro, thieves and other young criminals who needed to be imprisoned. Life was tough inside that fence with hundreds of cruel, wicked big boys. *But it's better than being eaten up,* Pedro thought with a shiver.

One tear slipped down his thin brown cheek as he scampered off to tell Alfredo the bad news.

Roman Mullet, the missionary, whistled a happy tune as he walked down the street. As usual, a crowd of ragged boys followed at his heels, hoping that this kind-faced American would give them something.

Roman loved children, and his heart went out to these poor young beggars on the streets of San Salvador. He had always had a kind word and a pocketful of coins to give them, but that seemed like so little. *At last!* Roman thought as he stopped at the heavy iron gate of the Boys' Observatory. *At last our new Children's Home is ready! Now we can take home some of the poor orphans in this city and give them proper love and care.*

"Here are the boys you are to take today," the principal of the Observatory said to Roman. "They are too young to live here, learning bad habits from our older boys. They will have much better care in your Children's Home. I don't know why they look so scared! Come on, boys," he scolded. "Be brave and behave yourselves! This Gringo will take good care of you."

But Pedro and Alfredo did not smile. Their eyes were full of fear as they were placed in the missionaries' car. "My name is Roman Mullet, but you can call me Papi, and this lady will be your Mami," said the missionary. "We are so happy you are coming home with us!" he smiled broadly.

Alfredo looked at the missionary's teeth and shivered.

"Poor little boys," Roman said softly to his wife Amanda in English. "They look so frightened! But we will soon cheer them up."

These white Gringos can't talk very well, Pedro thought. *They mix up their words like babies who are just learning to talk!* Pedro was right. Roman and Amanda Mullet had only been in El Salvador for a few years, so they were still learning how to speak Spanish.

When the two little boys arrived at their new home, they found it very different from the Observatory in the city. A pleasant, comfortable-looking house was ready for them, with clean soft beds, new clothes and even some toys to play with! Outside the house there was a big grassy yard and an orchard, with long rows of orange and lemon trees.

The Mullets already had a little girl named Rosa at the Children's Home, a beautiful brown-skinned toddler whom the police had found sitting alone on the sidewalk in a cardboard box. Then there was Jorge, a Salvadoran man who worked at the Home. His face was brown, too, and he spoke good Spanish! Alfredo felt a little bit better after he met Jorge.

Everyone at this new Children's Home was so kind and there was so much good food to eat! Little by little Pedro and Alfredo's fears slipped away. "Papi and Mami aren't going to eat us!" Pedro said boldly to the others one afternoon. "Those big boys were lying. It's *much* nicer here than at the Observatory!"

The boys grew happy and healthy, and sometimes they got into mischief.

"Señor Roman," Jorge complained to the missionary one day, "these boys use terrible language. We must teach them not to say such bad words! They must have learned them at the Observatory."

"What bad words are they saying?" Roman

asked in surprise. "I don't understand enough Spanish to catch them, I guess."

"Words like this," Jorge replied, and he mentioned a word which good children in El Salvador never use.

The word sounded strange to Roman's ears. As he walked away, he repeated it silently over and over to himself, so that he would not forget. *I must talk to the boys about this,* the missionary thought soberly.

That evening when he gathered the children together for family worship, Roman tried to explain to Pedro and Alfredo, why God wanted them to have clean hearts and clean speech. "The Lord is not pleased when we swear and use bad words," he told them. "We do not want you to say bad words like this any more, and we will try to help you break the habit. If you use such words again, we will need to punish you.

Pedro rolled his eyes meaningfully at Alfredo. They had already learned that "Papi Roman" kept a small strap hanging in his office and used it to spank boys who did not obey. "Yes, Papi," the boys agreed dutifully. "We won't say that word anymore!"

But in their hearts, the boys did not understand the seriousness of bad language. Using swear words made them feel big and tough, so they did not stop. During the next few days, there were several times when "Papi" needed to use the strap on boys who said bad words.

As Roman Mullet listened to the boys at their play, he kept watching out for that bad word Jorge had warned him about. He had repeated it in his mind so many times that he knew it by heart! Patiently he kept on trying to teach the children to use clean language and clean habits.

That Saturday, "Papi" and "Mami" took some of the children into town to do some shopping. "You ladies can buy your things, then wait for us in the park," Roman told his wife. "I'll take the boys to get new pants and then we will meet you there." Amanda, Rosa, and Carmen, a new girl at the Children's Home, climbed out of the car and disappeared among the crowd.

Pedro and Alfredo followed "Papi" into the shop where they were to buy new pants and then into a few more stores. Finally, laden with packages and bags, they walked back to the mission car. Laughing and talking, the two boys bounced around the back seat as Roman drove carefully down the crowded streets. In their excitement, they forgot to wonder where "Mami" and the girls were!

Roman, too, had forgotten about his wife. Whistling cheerfully, he guided the car along the highway leading out of town. Suddenly, as he stopped at a red light, the truth dawned upon him. He had left Amanda and the girls behind!

In his shock and confusion, Roman said the first thing that came to his mind. Unfortunately, that thing was the very same bad word which Jorge had taught him, the word he had tried so hard to remember! By repeating it over and over, he had fixed the word in his mind. Now, in his time of trouble, the word had slipped from his tongue! The missionary had said a bad word, and two little boys had heard him say it.

There was a strange silence in the car as Roman turned it around and headed back into the city.

"Lord, what shall I do now?" he prayed desperately.

Amanda and the girls were patiently waiting in the park. Roman helped them into the car and began the homeward trip once more. As he drove, he told his wife what had happened. Speaking softly in the language the children didn't understand, he asked, "What shall I do about it? Is my bad example going to ruin everything I've tried to teach these boys?"

"Better be honest with them," Amanda advised softly. "Talk about it, and let them see how sorry you are. Perhaps this will help them see how serious bad language is."

The two boys were very subdued when they reached their Children's Home. After all the bundles had been carried in from the car, Roman called them into his office.

"Boys," he began sorrowfully, "do you know why we are here?"

"No!" exclaimed Pedro, but he did not look at the missionary.

"We didn't do anything," Alfredo chimed in uneasily.

"Did *I* do something?" Roman questioned.

Pedro shook his head, looking only at the floor, but Alfredo was more honest. "Papi, you said that bad word," he answered.

"That's right, I did," Roman said sadly. "I said

that bad word you boys must never say. I didn't mean to, and I'm very sorry because God doesn't like us to talk that way. Now, you boys must punish me."

"How, Papi?" Alfredo asked fearfully.

"You must take that strap and spank me, while I kneel down here," Roman replied.

"Oh, no, Papi!" "No, Papi! We couldn't do that!" the boys cried out in horror.

"Then what shall we do?" asked the missionary soberly.

All at once the two little boys flung their arms around Roman. "Let's pray for you!" Alfredo cried tearfully. "Yes, Papi, Jesus will help you not to do it again," Pedro wept, as he hugged Roman tightly.

"All right, boys, we will ask Jesus to forgive me and help all three of us," the missionary agreed. Tears were running down his own cheeks as they knelt together.

This was the day Pedro and Alfredo learned their lesson. The bad word, which had seemed so tough and smart when boys said it, had sounded so very ugly when it came from the lips of their kind and godly "Papi"! The Mullets never heard either of the two boys use it again.

Historical Note:

This story happened in El Salvador in 1972. Roman and Amanda Mullet spent six and a half years in El Salvador. They founded a children's home called Nueva Vida Y Esperanza, which means New Life and Hope. Rosa, Pedro, and Alfredo were the first children to live there. Over the years many more children have been given loving care and Christian teaching in the Nueva Vida Y Esperanza Home.

Roman Mullet, a minister from Ohio, went to his eternal reward in the summer of 2004.

27

LOST !

"Come, Petrona, it's time to start out for home," Catarina called to her daughter. "Hurry! The sun is halfway down the sky, and we want to be home before it gets dark."

The brown-skinned Belizian woman tied her baby daughter Juana securely into the carrying-cloth on her back. "Thank you, and Goodbye," she shyly told the nurse, who had just finished caring for both of her daughters at the clinic.

Reluctantly, Petrona left the group of children she had been playing with, and followed her mother. It usually took about three hours to walk from the Crique Sarco Mission clinic back to their own village of Otexa... a long, weary journey. But nine-year-old Petrona understood the need for haste. She, too, wanted to get home before darkness fell!

The afternoon was hot and humid. Soon droplets of sweat trickled down Catarina's face and neck. Baby Juana, fussy and fretful from the shot she had received at the clinic, whimpered uneasily until at last she fell asleep on her mother's back. "I'm so thirsty, Mama!" Petrona began to complain, "when can I get a drink?"

"There will be a creek by the trail soon," Catarina replied. "You can take a drink there."

Silently, the three plodded along the path. Lush green vines, trees and flowers flourished on all sides in the moist heat. Tropical orchids, in every shade of pink, red and purple, bloomed from the crannies of the older trees, while smaller trees bore wild fruits: coconuts, May plums, and guavas. Bamboo canes grew thickly wherever they could find room, with their lovely sun-dappled leaves. A monkey called to his companion in the distance, and exotic birds flashed through the trees on business of their own.

But Catarina and Petrona scarcely saw the beauties of this wild bush country. Their minds were on their home and supper.

"I'm going to take this old short cut," Catarina suddenly announced. "We don't usually come this way. But it will save time!" Turning from the well-worn trail, she led Petrona off along another path. This trail looked like it had not been used very much in recent years. Vines and bamboo shoots were growing across the path, nearly hiding it from view.

"Now we should be home sooner," Catarina said with satisfaction. Mother and daughter began to walk more briskly along the shady, overgrown trail. It was slightly cooler under the trees, but Catarina soon found that the old path was hard to follow. Sharp bamboo spears kept stabbing her bare feet, and sometimes the trail was blocked completely by fallen logs. Sometimes she wasn't even sure where the path *was*! But she plodded on, and Petrona silently followed.

It seemed like they had been walking for hours, when suddenly the air darkened and a gust of wind whipped through the trees. "Mama, it's going to rain!" Petrona groaned.

Sure enough, great drops of rain began to fall. Soon the drops became a downpour, and the travellers left the trail to stand under a big tree. When the shower let up a little, though, Catarina was ready to leave their shelter and go on. "We have to hurry!" she worried. "It will soon be dark, and then I won't be able to see this trail!"

Baby Juana began to cry again as they trudged along through the drizzling rain. The path grew harder to find as the light faded slowly. Suddenly it came to an end, at the edge of a large open space. "Mama, this looks like a cornfield!" Petrona exclaimed. "See, the old stubble is still standing in rows, even though weeds are growing up in them."

"Yes, someone used to live around here, and this was their cornfield," Catarina agreed. "Now where can the trail be?" Hurrying through the cornfield, she found the path once more on the other side... or was it the path? Dusk was falling, and it was hard to be sure. *Maybe I should have stayed with the regular trail,* Catarina thought fearfully. Hurrying, she forced her tired legs to move on.

"Mama, it's getting dark," Petrona spoke in a small voice. "Yes, I know. Walk faster," was all her mother replied. Mosquitoes appeared in great clouds as the sun went down. Petrona waved her arms in all directions, quietly slapping the ones that zoomed in to land on her. There was no use complaining, she knew. All could do was hurry, to get out of these woods before darkness brought snakes and jaguars out of their hiding places. *Jaguars!* Petrona shivered and moved faster.

Hungry, thirsty, and so tired, the three pushed on. When darkness fell, it was completely dark. There is no darkness on earth so black as the darkness of a tropical night in Belize, when rain clouds blot out the moon and stars! Bravely, Catarina kept on trying to find her way along the trail. Feeling with her hands and bare feet, she moved slowly through the dense jungle. All at once, she stopped in surprise. "What is this?" She cried out softly. "It feels like..."

"It's cornstalks, Mama," Petrona whispered. "We're in the cornfield again! How could we be?"

"We must have gone in a circle," Catarina groaned in despair. "We're lost. It's no use; I can't follow that old trail in the dark. All we can do is stay here and wait till morning!"

Feeling around for a smooth spot on the ground, Catarina and Petrona sat down close together. The mother lifted her baby from the carrying cloth on her back, and cuddled her in her arms. Silently the three sat listening to the sounds of the night: the whining mosquitoes, the faint crackling as a small animal moved close by, and the call of a night bird. Far away Petrona heard a cry, and fear prickled along her backbone. Could that have been a jaguar?

But Catarina was hearing something else. *Chug-chug-chug-chug...* sounded the distant rumble of a motor.

"Listen!" she whispered. "Do you hear that, Petrona? It's the generator at Crique Sarco. The machine they use to make electric lights for the mission. We must not be *too* far away! Maybe only two or three kilometers, straight."

She stirred restlessly, slapping at a mosquito. "If we could just walk straight toward the sound..." she said thoughtfully.

"Oh, Mama, no!" cried Petrona. "I'm so tired, and it's too dark to walk!"

Catarina sat in silence for a moment, considering. Then, abruptly, she made her decision. Rising to her feet, she placed the sleeping Juana in her older sister's lap. "I'll go by myself," she stated. "If I am alone, I can run. I will get to the mission quickly, and bring back men with lights. We can spend the night at the mission, where we will be safe!"

Tears streamed down Petrona's cheeks. "Mama, don't go!" she whimpered.

"Yes, that will be the best way," her mother replied firmly. "You stay right here, and don't make a sound. Try to keep Juana quiet, too, so nothing will..." she stopped. "Pray to God," she added softly, and vanished into the black night.

Through the darkness, the desperate mother ran like a deer, her hands always outstretched before her to feel for trees and other obstacles that might block her way. Surely the noise she made, as she crashed blindly through the bushes, would scare away any snakes or jaguars that might be lurking there? Straining her ears to hear that *chug-chug-chug* of the generator, she followed the sound. In the inky blackness of the night, there was no way to watch where she stepped! Many times poor Catarina moaned with pain as a sharp bamboo shoot stabbed into one of her bare feet. Twice she tripped and fell headlong to the ground, but there was nothing to do but get up and keep going. She had to get help to find her children, and quickly!

The clock in the mission house showed 10:30 when Alvin Schlabach heard the knock on his door. There stood a woman he had seen at the clinic earlier in the day, but how different she looked now! Her dress was torn in several places, and her bare feet were bleeding from many cuts.

"Help me, Mr. Alvin!" Catarina cried tearfully. "My children are lost in the bush!"

Hastily the missionary led the tired woman to a chair, while his wife Irene brought a fresh drink and bandages for her cut feet. After hearing Catarina's story, Alvin put on his boots and picked up his most powerful flashlight.

"I will get some men together, and we will go look for the girls," he assured Catarina. "You stay here. I will take Juan Choc along; he knows all the bush country around here. He will know exactly where that old cornfield would be!" Alvin turned to his wife. "Pray for us," he told her. With a smile and a wave, he was gone.

In a very short time, the missionary had a group of men ready to go. There were two health workers from the clinic, the Belizean Christian Juan Choc, and another man named Nicholas. *My, this is a black night,* Alvin thought as he followed the beam of the flashlight Juan carried. *I would soon be lost myself, if it weren't for Juan and the others!* He pictured a little girl out in this darkness, alone except for her baby sister, and shuddered. *There are snakes out here, and vampire bats, and jaguars!* "Lord, please protect those poor children, and help us to find them soon," he prayed silently.

Juan Choc was an expert hunter and tracker in the bush, and he followed the old, almost invisible trail easily. By midnight, the men had found the cornfield. But the overgrown field was empty— only rows of dead corn stubble and weeds showed in the flashlights' beams.

"Petrona! Petrona, where are you?" the men called. They fanned out across the whole field, searching carefully for the missing children. Could the girls be asleep? What had happened?

"They aren't in this field," Juan announced in frustration. "And this is the only old cornfield in the area. I don't know what to do now." He began to circle slowly around the field, looking for clues.

"Petrona! Where are you, Petrona?" Alvin

called. "Petrona!" shouted the other men. Suddenly, out of the distant blackness came an answering call. "Over here!"

"That was a man's voice, not a child's," Alvin exclaimed. "Who else would be out here on such a night?" "Who's there?" Juan shouted.

Again the voice answered faintly. "Over here!"

Out of the cornfield and through the bush, Alvin and his friends followed the strange voice. Whenever they called, the man's voice would reply. Keeping alert for snakes, the five searchers pressed through the thick bamboo and vines. "Over here! Come this way!" the strange voice sounded closer. "The children are here!"

"Who do you suppose he is?" Alvin asked Nicholas. "It sounds like he has found the girls!" "I don't know, but we will find out in a moment," the other man replied. "We're almost there."

"Over here!" the voice called one last time, and then there was silence, followed by the sleepy wail of a baby.

"Petrona! Juana!" Alvin shouted.

"Here I am!" came a small, frightened voice. Swinging his powerful light toward the sound, Juan saw the children at last. Huddled on the ground under a tree, Petrona still held her baby sister in her arms. Both children were speckled with mosquito bites, cold and sleepy and thirsty... but safe.

Gently, Alvin picked up the baby. "How did you girls get so far away from the cornfield?" he asked Petrona. "I thought I heard a jaguar," the little girl confessed. "I was scared, and I just ran till I couldn't go anymore."

"Where's the man who was with you?" Juan demanded, shining his light around through the trees.

"There wasn't anyone else with me," Petrona answered sleepily, clinging to the missionary's friendly hand. "Not any man at all!"

"But we heard a man calling," Nicholas insisted. "Where are you?" he shouted.

The other men called repeatedly, but there was no reply.

"Nobody's here," said Juan at last. "But we all heard his voice. Do you think..." he stopped.

In the silent darkness, a feeling of awe and reverence swept over Alvin. Surely, God was near! "It must have been an angel," he spoke softly. "God sent an angel to protect the children, and be with them until they were found."

Historical Note:

This story happened near Crique Sarco, Belize, in 1992. Catarina, Petrona and Juana spent a few days at the clinic to have their bites and cuts treated, then the missionaries took them safely home to their own village.

Alvin Schlabach is an American missionary pastor in Crique Sarco at the time of this writing. He and his wife Irene had been in Belize for just a year when this incident happened.

28

THROUGH WATER AND FIRE

It was 35 degrees below zero. Icy cold gripped the forests and lakes of Northern Ontario, Canada, in an iron fist. It was a good day for staying comfortably beside your fireplace or heating stove! But the two men on the mission snowmobile had a job to do, and they needed a cold day to do it.

"There goes a moose!" Morley Meekis, the Indian driver of the snowmobile, shouted above the engine's roar. His alert dark eyes had seen the huge shadowy figure before it melted back into the forest.

"Well, there's the tractor," the second man replied with a grin. Alvin Frey, the missionary, knew he would probably never be so wise in the ways of the Northwoods as the Cree Indians to whom he preached. But he did have many new things to show them!

When Alvin had arrived at the Deer Lake Mission a few years before, he found the Cree Indians there living in deep poverty. All their food supplies, except for what meat and fish they hunted for themselves, had to be purchased at high prices from the trading post. Deer Lake was over a hundred miles from any road, so supplies were expensive. Most Indian families made less than one thousand dollars a year, so when hunting was poor they had little to fall back on. In despair, many of the men spent their last cent on whiskey, to drink and forget their hungry families for a few hours.

How could Alvin show these people that Jesus cared about them? How could he help them to help themselves? Both questions had found one answer in the tractor which now stood under a crude shed at the edge of the woods. Christians in the East who were concerned about the mission to the Indians had raised money to buy the tractor. This machine was the first tractor ever seen by the Indians of Deer Lake, and it had made a big difference in their lives. Several acres of woodland had been cleared with the tractor and Alvin had shown the Indians how to plant potatoes for themselves. Soon the garden was producing tons of potatoes and turnips for the village of Deer Lake!

The garden patch was on an island, across the lake from the village. During the summer, the tractor had to stay on the island; but now that Deer Lake had frozen over, Alvin was going to drive it back across the ice. All the people of the village were eagerly waiting for their turn to use the tractor for hauling firewood.

"Better measure the ice again on this side," Morley advised. Taking his axe, he began chopping a hole in the frozen surface of the lake. Meanwhile, Alvin fueled up the tractor and prepared to start the engine.

When the two men were satisfied that all was ready, Alvin started the tractor. The engine roared into life, with clouds of exhaust smoke hanging in the frosty air. "Are you coming?" he called over his shoulder to Morley, as the tractor chugged slowly out onto the ice.

"Soon as I can get my Skidoo going," the Indian shouted, bending over his snowmobile. For some reason, the machine was slow to start. Sinking back onto the seat to rest for a moment, Morley watched Alvin and the tractor proceeding across the frozen lake.

Suddenly a horrible, threatening CRACK! sounded through the distant ice! Morley gasped and stood staring as the rear end of the tractor lurched sharply and began to sink. Somewhere beneath the ice, a flowing current of water had worn a thin spot in the frozen surface. And Alvin, with the tractor, had hit that thin spot!

"Help! Oh, God, help him!" Morley cried out as he tried frantically to start his own engine. Out on the lake, both tractor and missionary sank through the hole and were gone.

Pinned beneath the steering wheel of the sinking vehicle, Alvin Frey struggled vainly to free himself. The shock of the freezing cold water soaking through his thick clothes almost made him cry out in pain, but he instinctively held his breath as his head went under.

Down, down into the dark depths sank the heavy tractor. Ten feet... twenty feet... thirty... forty. As the tractor's tires touched the muddy bottom fifty feet from the surface of the lake, Alvin finally managed to free himself from the seat.

Hurry! Swim back up! Alvin told himself, but his winter clothes and boots weighed him down. His body was becoming starved for oxygen after several minutes underwater. *Don't breathe the water, or you'll drown... don't breathe!,* his mind warned dimly. With painful slowness he rose toward the surface.

Fuzzy thoughts and pictures began to whirl dizzily through his fading brain. *What will my family do if I don't make it? My wife Lydianne... my children. And all the Indians here at Deer Lake Mission! Oh, why did I lose the tractor?*

With a gentle bump, Alvin's head hit a sheet of ice. Hope flared quickly, only to be replaced by despair. *If I've come up under the ice, I'll never get out,* the missionary thought. *Well, I'm ready to die... Lord, here I come!*

Suddenly the broken cake of ice floated away, and Alvin's head shot out into the air! Frantically he breathed and breathed, gulping great lungs-full of oxygen into his aching body. His dazzled eyes took in the beauty of the sunlit trees and sparkling snow, but for a fleeting moment Alvin felt a stab of disappointment. *Heaven was so close! he thought. I was almost there. Another moment and*

I would have seen my Lord Jesus.

Brrrrr-m! A motor roared nearby, as Morley Meekis arrived on his snowmobile just in time to pull the dripping missionary onto a solid patch of ice.

"Oh, Brother Alvin— you're alive!" cried the Indian, his dark face wet with tears. "You were under the water for ten minutes. I thought there was no hope!"

He hurried Alvin onto the snowmobile, and the two men sped away. It was another mile and a half back to the village. By the time they stopped in front of the trading post, Alvin's wet clothing had frozen to solid ice. Unable to move his arms or legs, the missionary allowed himself to be carried into the warm store.

"Talk, Alvin!" shouted his Indian friends, beating with their fists on the icy shell around his body. "Are you all right? Talk to us!"

Breathlessly, the missionary laughed. "Calm down," he said. "I'm all right! Just let Morley tell you all about it, while I get warm."

When he had heard the story, an old Indian wisely nodded his wrinkled head. "Now I know *this* white man tells the truth," he said solemnly. "Or else he would never have come out of that water alive!"

Three weeks later, the police put a trained diver on a plane and sent him to the mission. Wearing a special wet suit, the man dived to the lake bottom and fastened a cable around the axle of the tractor. Soon the mission tractor was back on the job!

As the months passed, Alvin began to understand one reason, at least, why God had allowed the tractor to fall through the ice. When Christians throughout the country learned of what had happened, they made new efforts to support the mission work. In church after church, as the story was told of Alvin Frey's narrow escape, many people pledged to send money for the missions among the Cree Indians.

Six years slipped by, as Alvin Frey and his family continued their work with Northern Light Gospel Mission. He never forgot the day God had spared his life in the freezing lake. And then came a morning when Alvin's faith was to be tested by fire as well!

The weather was cold once more and Alvin needed to keep the furnace going in the basement of the mission house. "Looks like it's gone out," he observed one morning, poking around in the ashes of the dead fire. "I'll need to use some of this!" Reaching for a bottle of old diesel fuel, he squirted some into the logs piled in the firebox.

WHOOOMP! With a sound like ripping cloth, the diesel fluid exploded into the air. The bottle blew up in Alvin's hand, spraying fuel all over Alvin, turning him into a human torch before he could react to what was happening! Flames sprang up all over the basement.

"Oh, no! I'm on fire!" the horrified missionary screamed.

Seizing the first blanket he could find, Alvin rolled himself into it to smother the flames. Quick as he was, though, the fire had already eaten into his face, arms, and chest. Loose, shriveled skin hung in shreds from his blackened body as Lydianne came running to meet him at the head of the stairs.

"We've got to put that fire out!" Alvin gasped. For the next fifteen minutes, the couple ran back and forth with buckets of water from the kitchen. Not until the fire was doused, and the mission house safe, did Alvin take time to think of his own burned body.

"You'll have to go to the hospital," his wife declared, and Alvin reluctantly agreed. Across the frozen lake at the trading post, the mission nurse radioed for a helicopter.

"The helicopter is at God's Lake and can't get to you," a voice on the radio replied. "A storm is moving in. But Whitey Hostetler can come pick up your patient and fly him to Red Lake. Have the Indians choose a place where he can land on the ice, and mark it with cedar branches!"

Storm clouds were gathering. Soon the air would be filled with whirling snow, making flight impossible. Would Whitey, the pilot, be able to get the injured missionary to Red Lake in time? As Alvin lay in the schoolhouse beside the lake, his burned face and body grew steadily more painful. Dimly through the agonized throbbing, he knew that dozens of Indians were coming and going beside the cot where he lay. The Christian Indians, members of his congregation, were taking turns coming in to pray over their missionary.

Out on the ice, more men worked to mark a landing place for Whitey's small plane. "The ice isn't safe," one worried to his neighbor. "It really isn't thick enough to land a plane on!"

The pilot himself had come to the same conclusion. "I won't be able to make a complete stop," he radioed to the Deer Lake villagers. "Have Alvin waiting on the ice, and be ready to help him in as I come past!"

Snow was starting to fall as two strong Indians trudged onto the frozen lake, carrying the injured missionary between them in a blanket. "The plane's coming!" a boy shouted from the bank. A motor whined, and the small three-seater aircraft flew over the trees. Making a tight circle, Whitey sailed the plane down toward the waiting group. His pontoons barely touched the weak ice as he throttled back the engine. "Ready... set... go!" one Indian chanted. Holding open the passenger door with one hand, Whitey skimmed alongside. At just the right instant the Indians dashed forward, shoving Alvin into the plane. "Got him!" cheered the watching crowd, as the door closed and the plane zoomed off across the lake.

Just then there was a howl of wind and the storm descended in all its fury. "Ten minutes later would have been too late," dark-skinned Morley muttered to a friend. "Let's go home and pray some more."

After Alvin reached Red Lake, he was put into a larger plane for the flight to the hospital in Winnipeg. It was evening before he was admitted to the hospital's burn unit. The masked doctors and nurses shook their heads as they worked with salves and bandages. "This is a bad one," a nurse whispered to her companion. "He'll be here a long time!"

As Alvin lay suffering in his quiet bed that evening, he thought bitterly of the morning's events. *How could I have been so stupid?* he scolded himself. *What a dumb thing to do, and cause all this trouble for everybody!*

Suddenly a quiet figure stood at his bedside, face covered by a hospital mask. "Do you know me, Alvin?" came a woman's voice. It was Sadie Yoder, a missionary who worked in Winnipeg. Softly she prayed over Alvin, and then slipped out of the room again. A few minutes later another Christian came in. "Brother Alvin, you and I never met before," this man said cheerfully. "But the Lord told me to come in and pray for you tonight!" Laying his hands lightly on Alvin's head, he began to speak with God.

While the stranger prayed, Alvin felt his bitterness melt away. From disgust at himself, his attitude changed to joy. *In everything give thanks,* he thought. *Yes, that verse means even this! I can still rejoice in the Lord. Oh, so many people have been praying for me. All my Indians at Deer Lake... I didn't know they cared for me so much. And now Sadie and this brother whose name I don't even know. Thank You, Lord, for all this love!*

As Alvin's spirits lifted, he felt something happening in his face, too. The pain was fading away, and he could sense a difference in the way his skin felt. Soothed and sleepy, he drifted off into a refreshing slumber.

In the morning, a nurse came to change Alvin's

bandages. As the last strips of gauze fell away from his face, she gasped in surprise. "Didn't you just come in last night?" the nurse exclaimed. "Your face is already healed! This is impossible!" The burns on Alvin's body took a little longer to heal, but still he was ready to be dismissed from the hospital in record time. Before he left, the head nurse came back to shake his hand. "Mr. Frey, I hope you realize that this was a miracle," she stated. "Most people with burns as bad as yours need to be in the hospital for at least six weeks!" Alvin's face lit up in a radiant smile. His bushy eyebrows still had not grown back completely, but very few scars remained from his trial by fire. "God is great," he told the nurse simply. "And I had a lot of people speaking to Him for me!"

Historical Note:

Alvin Frey worked for 20 years with the Northern Light Gospel Mission. He fell through the ice on the tractor in 1963 and the fire occurred in 1969. With his wife and five children— Paul, Larry, Steve, Calvin, and Ruthann— he has remained in the Lord's work in Canada.

At the time of this writing, he is the pastor of a church in Manitoba.

Conclusion

UNCLE RALPH AND THE MOOSE

Timmy had finished eating his potatoes and placed his fork neatly at the edge of his plate. While the rest of the Miller family talked over their day's happenings, he sat silently, lost in thought.

"Why doesn't anyone from *our* church ever go to be a missionary in other countries?" he asked suddenly.

All the Millers turned to look at Timmy in surprise.

"Why, Timmy, what do you mean?" Dad said.

"Well, all these stories Mom has been telling us..." he hesitated. "There should be missionaries from our church, too, shouldn't there?"

"You're right, Timmy," his father replied. "God

expects each one of us who believe in Jesus to be a missionary. Some of us are missionaries here, where we live right now. But there are people among our own family and friends who have gone to foreign countries to be missionaries, too!"

"How about Uncle Steve and Aunt Rosa and the cousins?" Mama suggested. "They are missionaries in Ireland, you know. And Brother Ron Border and his family, remember how they spent a year in France?"

"Don't forget Sister Brenda," Peter spoke up. "She was your teacher when you were in first grade, Timmy, and now she has gone to Belize to teach children there! She's the one who sent us the story about Petrona and the angel."

"And there's Miriam Sommers, too," Sharon added. "She lives way, far over in Kenya with the mission there."

"Your Grandpa William McGrath might be the *busiest* missionary in our church," Mama went on with a smile. "He has started mission churches in Costa Rica, Ireland, and New Mexico. He spent two years teaching and preaching in Alaska, and he still travels all over the United States to preach. Tonight he will be preaching in Oregon, and we must not forget to pray for him."

"Tonight, Timmy, you will be seeing another real, live missionary," Dad stated. "After supper we are planning to go visit Great-Grandma Alice, and you can meet him at her house!"

"Who?" "Who is it?" all four Miller children asked at once. Their parents smiled mysteriously. "Wait and see," was all Dad would say.

When the Millers walked into Great-Grandma Alice's house an hour later, a smiling man and woman rose from the couch to greet them. Peter and Timmy stared at the couple. *I know I've seen them before,* Peter thought. "It's Uncle Ralph and Aunt Carolyn!" Sharon squealed happily. "My, we haven't seen you for several years!"

"Yes, it's been a long time," Aunt Carolyn said, coming forward to kiss her niece. "I don't suppose your younger children remember us at all. And we've never seen this one... is this Laura?"

"Children, this is my Aunt Carolyn and Uncle Ralph," their mother explained to the Miller children. "So they are *your* great-aunt and great-uncle, and they are missionaries in Canada."

Laura gazed wide-eyed at these relatives whom she had never seen before. Real, live missionaries, just like in Mama's stories! She climbed onto her mother's lap as the family took seats around Great-Grandma's cozy living room.

"Well, Ralph, why don't you tell these children some stories?" Great-Grandma suggested briskly.

"You boys would probably like to hear about a plane crash, wouldn't you?" Uncle Ralph chuckled, looking at Peter and Timmy as they sat side by side on Great-Grandma's big leather footstool. "I spent many years as a bush pilot, flying planes for the Northern Light Gospel Mission," he went on. "The Cree Indians used to call me 'Mbimish-say-wininni', which means 'Man who flies'. All the mission stations were built on the shores of lakes, deep in the wild woods of Western Ontario. Most of them could not be reached by any

197

road, so the only way to bring in people or supplies was by airplane. I used to say, 'I fly everything, even kitchen sinks!' Quite a few times I had to carry live goats in my plane, so that missionaries' children would have fresh milk to drink."

"How did goats behave in an airplane?" Peter was curious.

"Well, I tied them fast and piled hay bales around them," Uncle Ralph replied, "and they flew more quietly than some people do!

"We lived at the Red Lake mission and I was almost home one evening when the trouble started. I was flying a little Cessna-180, with two fuel tanks, one in each wing. Usually when one tank got empty, I had only to flip a switch and start using gas from the other tank. But that evening, when I tried to switch tanks, my engine sputtered and died in midair. Somehow the carburetor had become air-locked, which kept the fuel from flowing into the engine. Now, boys, can you guess what happens if an airplane engine stops when you are in the air?"

"I suppose you'd come down," Timmy answered.

"Yes, there was only one way to go and that was DOWN!" Uncle Ralph continued. "Landing on a lake would have been the best thing to do, but there were no lakes near enough. I was only fifteen hundred feet up, and rapidly losing altitude. Another experienced bush pilot had once given me this advice: "If you ever need to crash-land your plane in the trees, pick the *thickest* trees around!' I thought of his words now as I tried to guide the sinking plane.

"Ahead was a spot where the tops of the Jack Pine trees looked thick and fairly level. Carefully I banked the plane around and aimed it toward that spot. Down, down glided the plane, till it was almost touching the trees. *Lord, this is up to You!* I prayed hastily as I pulled back on the controls. Swish! Crackle! The pontoons began to chop through the treetops. *I guess I could get hurt!* I remember thinking as the Cessna descended into the trees with an awful crashing and snapping of broken branches. Bang! One propeller hit a tree trunk and stopped. Slowly, the plane tilted and settled down between trees with the tip of one pontoon float touching the ground, and all was quiet.

"I was still strapped into my seat, and completely unhurt. Not even a scratch! I bowed my head in a prayer of thanksgiving. Then unbuckling my seat belt, I climbed out the door and down to the pontoon. From there, I could jump to the ground.

"It was already 6:30 in the evening and we usually didn't fly after dark. So I knew I would need to wait until morning for rescue. I gathered dry wood and made a fire to cook some food from my emergency kit. Darkness fell as I sat by my campfire, and I felt very small and alone there in that wild forest!

"Suddenly I heard a sound that made me snap to attention. A large animal was coming through the trees. HUMPF! HUMPF! came a grunting call, and I knew just what it meant. A bull moose was walking around not far away! It was September, mating season for the moose, and a bull would be dangerous. Every bull moose jealously guarded his territory against strangers, and I could not expect any mercy from this one! A bull moose might weigh twelve hundred pounds. Even the Indians stayed far away from them in September!

"Quickly putting out my fire, I swung myself back up onto the pontoon hanging down from the plane. Climbing into the plane, I unrolled my sleeping bag as well as I could and prepared to spend the night up there.

"HUMPF! HUMPF!" the challenging grunt sounded again from below. I had climbed up to safety just in time! Angrily, the huge moose threw back his head and bellowed like a bull. I shivered. *Sorry, old fellow. I didn't mean to crash into your territory!* I thought. As the night wore on, the bull moose kept tramping back and forth through the woods beneath my plane, as if he hoped that I would come down. About every half hour, he bellowed horribly again. It was midnight before he finally gave up and went crashing away, allowing me to get some sleep."

"What happened next? How did you get home?" Peter wondered.

"In the morning," Uncle Ralph went on, "I climbed down from the plane with an axe, a compass and some matches. Using the compass, I began walking North, toward the nearest lake. With my axe, I chopped a nick in some of the trees I passed, to mark a trail back to where the plane hung in the trees. It was only a mile and a half to the lake, but those woods were so thick that the hike took three hours! I found blueberries to eat along the way, though. And was I ever thankful that I didn't meet my enemy, the moose!

"When I reached the lake shore, I made a big fire, with lots of smoke. Soon a rescue plane spotted my signal from the air, and I was safely on my way home. Later we were able to return for my airplane, drag it to the lake, repair it, and fly it away again."

The Miller children stared at Uncle Ralph, their faces filled with awe. Such an adventure! What other stories might this man have to tell?

"How many years did you spend with the Northern Light Gospel Mission?" Sharon asked.

"Thirty-two years," the strongly-built missionary replied. "I have been a pilot for most of those years, and in 1982 I was ordained to the ministry, too."

"Did you know Alvin Frey up there in Canada?" asked Peter. "Mom told us some stories about him."

"Yes, we worked together with Alvin, too," Uncle Ralph answered. "Your Aunt Carolyn was the nurse who took care of him when he was burned, on the airplane trip from Red Lake to the big city hospital. We were both along on that trip, to take him to Winnipeg. Did your mother tell you about the time his tractor fell through the ice, too?"

"Yes, she did!" the Miller children nodded. "His life has been spared by God more than once," Uncle Ralph said solemnly, "and so has mine. A missionary's life involves some danger and adventure, and a lot of just plain hard work. I don't know what God has planned for you children! But if you follow His leading, you will always be glad you

201

did. There is no better place to be than the place where the Lord calls you."

Historical Note:
Uncle Ralph in this story is Ralph Hartman, of Ear Falls, Ontario. At the time of this writing he has been a missionary to the Cree Indians for 32 years. He is the author's uncle.

Acknowledgments

Chapter 1 is based on an incident recorded in the book Out of the Jaws of the Lion*, Homer E. Dowdy (Harper & Row)

Chapter 3 is adapted from the book The Small Woman * by Alan Burgess Chapter 4 is based on material from Trail Maker— the Story of David Livingstone, R.O. Latham (Christian Literature Crusade) and A Guessing Book— David Livingstone, Fern Neal Stocher (Moody Press)

Chapter 5 is adapted from the book Escape From New Age Materialism, Ludlow Walker (Harbor House) by the author's permission

Chapter 6 is based on an incident from Heroes of the South Seas *, Martha Burbanks (American Tract Society.)

Chapter 8 is based on an incident from Hudson Taylor's Spiritual Secret, Dr. & Mrs. Howard Taylor (Moody Press)

Chapter 9 is adapted from Annals of the Redeemed, Anna Talbot McPherson (Allegheny Publications) by the author's permission.

Chapter 10 Based on accounts in the book Peril by Choice, James C. Hefley (Zondervan Publishing House)

Chapter 11 Based on material from the book Through Gates of Splendor Elisabeth Elliot (Tyndale House Publishers)

Chapter 13 Based on material from Forty Missionary Stories* and I Heard Good News Today, Cornelia Lehn (Faith & Life Press)

Chapter 14 Based on an incident from Into the Glory, Jamie Buckingham (Wycliffe)

Chapter 16 Based on incidents from Jungle Harvest, Ruby Scott (Baptist Home Missionary Society)

Chapter 17 Adapted from Awaiting the Dawn, Dorcas Hoover (Christian Light Publications) by author's permission.

Chapter 18 Based on incidents from The Untold Korea Story*, Pierce Anderson (Zondervan Publishing House)

Chapter 19 Based on material from Forty Missionary Stories* and Who Was Who in Church History, Elgin S. Mover (Keats Publishing)

Chapter 20 Sources include: A Chance to Die, Elisabeth Elliot (Fleming Revell) and Amy Carmichael— Let the Little Children Come, Lois H. Dick (Moody Press)

Chapter 21 Based on an incident from Transformed Europeans *by Robert Evans

Chapter 22 Based on information in Day of Disaster*, Katie Wieke (Herald Press)

Chapter 23 Based on an incident in Giants of the Missionary Trail, Eugene M. Harrison (Prairie Bible Institute

Chapter 24 Based on the account in Thinking Africa* by Raymond Bush Chapter 25 Adapted from the book A Sower went Forth, Martha Palmer (Rod & Staff Publishers) by permission from the author

* Not in Print

Also by Mildred A. Martin:

Storytime with the Millers
Valuable lessons for children ages 4-8

Prudence and the Millers
Stories and Scripture lessons on courtesy,
health and safety. Ages 7-14

Prudence and Your Health
Workbook to accompany *Prudence and
the Millers*. Ages 9-12

School Days with the Millers
The Miller children live and learn valuable lessons—
at school and at home. Ages 7-14

Wisdom and the Millers
(Proverbs for Children)
25 chapters illustrating great truths of life in
story form. Ages 6-13

La Sabiduría y la familia Miller
Wisdom and the Millers in Spanish

Working with Wisdom
Workbook for *Wisdom and the Millers*. Ages 7-10

Make and Do with the Millers
Creativity and coloring for preschoolers

Inquire at your favorite book dealer or write to:

Green Pastures Press
50 Green Pastures Lane
Mifflin, PA 17058
United States of America
Email: greenpastures@emypeople.net